WAKING UP IN AMERICA

WAKING UP IN AMERICA

CARTOONS BY TED RALL

ST. MARTIN'S PRESS/NEW YORK

SPECIAL THANKS TO: JUDY S. CHANG, JEAN + STAN ARNOLD, EDITH HOLSINGER, KIM VOGEL, ALEX KUCZYNSKI, BILL TAYLOR AND TAMARA JONES. NON, MAMAN, JE NE T'AI PAS OUBLIÉ! MEGA ULTRA SUPER THANX TO DAN HASSAN FOR THE TITLE AND DISGUSTING ATTITUDE.

LIBRARY OF CONGRESS CATALOGING-IN-PUBLICATION DATA

Rall, Ted.
Waking up in America / Ted Rall.
p. cm.
ISBN 0-312-08518-4
1. American wit and humor. I. Title.
PN6161.R34 1992
741.5'973--dc20

92-19512
CIP

FIRST EDITION: SEPTEMBER 1992

10 9 8 7 6 5 4 3 2 1

"WHAT'S WRONG WITH YOU IS WHAT'S WRONG TODAY."

—New York Dolls, 1973

Everyone in this country has their problems wrapped up in neat little packages. Like yours, my dysfunctions are standard issue. I was born a few months before the assassination of John F. Kennedy, just one more birth statistic in the largest birth year in American history. My generation's childhoods were characterized by shattered families, overcrowded classrooms, dismal pop culture, and menial jobs, all against a backdrop of national cynicism inspired by Vietnam and Watergate. My foray into the frenzy of mid-1980s corporatism was marked by a series of deferred or artificial promotions. There are a lot of us competing for the same slice of economic pie—it's hard to accept that older Baby Boomers have already gobbled it all.

My mother and father are divorced, as are the parents of two-thirds of my peers. I grew up in Dayton, Ohio, a rust-belt town that called itself America's most average city. Like many Midwesterners, I moved to a *real* city—in my case, New York—only to discover that you never really escape the Midwest. A suburban upbringing lurks somewhere behind your optic nerve, waiting for a random moment on a late-night subway to strike as raw urban paranoia. I'm white and lower-middle class. Sometimes I find it hard to understand those who aren't. If any of this stuff gives you any insight while reading my cartoons, please let me know—reader input saves on therapy.

I like to suffer loudly. The American Experiment is failing, but nobody can face reality. Those who point out our problems are called unpatriotic, paranoid, or ungrateful. Journalists and politicians marginalize social critics by defining the norm in terms that are unrecognizable to the average citizen. These cultural propagandists have convinced those unwilling or unable to conform that they are weak and therefore irrelevant. Truth is defined by a monolithic majority. Thinking has become a group activity.

Young adults are struggling to be heard over a din of 1960s nostalgia. Media pundits call us "twentysomethings"—a neo Lost Generation of Americans born after 1960. We have been politically, socially, and economically deleted from the social contract. The aging Baby Boomers and the elderly who run the corporations, government, and cultural institutions declare that we have nothing to say; the obvious corollary is that no one should listen to us. Magazines tell us that the concept of youth has become flexible, that the Boomers' economic prowess makes "young" and "hip" whatever age they happen to be. They're wrong. The Rolling Stones, Cher, and George Bush may be mainstream, but they're not young. When middle-aged people usurp the role of youth, they stifle economic and cultural progress and wind up looking ridiculous. My generation desperately needs role models; instead, we're embarrassed by our elders.

American youth has always been disposable as war fodder and cheap labor, but the 1980s added a new wrinkle to this historic exploitation—even the "best and brightest" became fair game for abuse. Young adults who followed the rules of the postwar economy—earn good grades in school, attend a prestigious university, work in a large corporation, and retire well—got screwed. Financial aid vanished overnight. Brilliant young people were hired to work as secretaries and clerks. Aging Boomers relied on the strength of their number to silence the new generation just as they had used it to exert influence twenty years ago. The current Not-So-Great Depression has reduced America's cities to a mass of crumbling WPA concrete, while overpaid executives lay off younger workers. Eighty-five percent of the jobs lost to date since the post-1987 economic collapse belonged to workers under twenty-five years of age. America no longer has any use for its young—not even to exploit them. I watched on TV as inner-city blacks burned down Los Angeles a few weeks ago. Maybe they've hit upon something there.

The politics of exclusion cannot prevent young people from drawing cartoons—only from publishing them. Hundreds of gifted artists with important things to say persevere throughout the United States. At this writing, a few have published books or obtained syndication contracts. But it's not nearly enough. I wish that all musicians, authors, bankers, mayors, professors, and cartoonists were under thirty. If the current state of America is a good indication, its aged ruling class could use a rest.

Many older artists continue to contribute important voices to cartooning. I owe much to visionaries like Jules Feiffer, Mike Peters, Wayne Stayskal, and Matt Groening, who remain relevant and vibrant by continuously striving to adapt to new conditions and starting new trends. I don't hope I'll die before I get old. I want to get old just like them.

Ted Rall
New York City
May 20, 1992

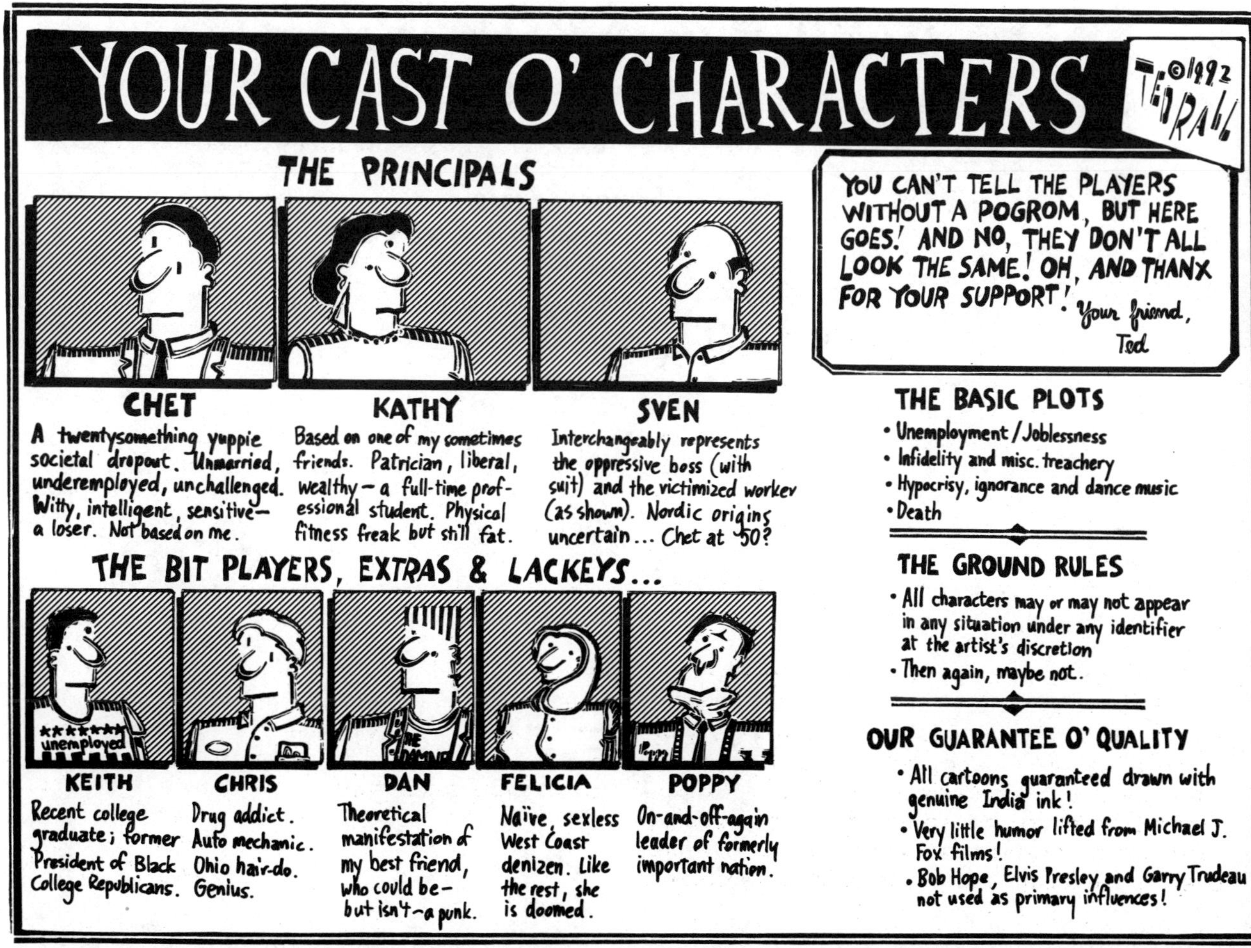
YOUR CAST O' CHARACTERS
©1992 TED RALL
THE PRINCIPALS
YOU CAN'T TELL THE PLAYERS WITHOUT A POGROM, BUT HERE GOES! AND NO, THEY DON'T ALL LOOK THE SAME! OH, AND THANX FOR YOUR SUPPORT! Your friend, Ted
CHET
A twentysomething yuppie societal dropout. Unmarried, underemployed, unchallenged. Witty, intelligent, sensitive— a loser. Not based on me.
KATHY
Based on one of my sometimes friends. Patrician, liberal, wealthy— a full-time professional student. Physical fitness freak but still fat.
SVEN
Interchangeably represents the oppressive boss (with suit) and the victimized worker (as shown). Nordic origins uncertain... Chet at 50?
THE BASIC PLOTS
• Unemployment / Joblessness
• Infidelity and misc. treachery
• Hypocrisy, ignorance and dance music
• Death
THE BIT PLAYERS, EXTRAS & LACKEYS...
unemployed
KEITH
Recent college graduate; former President of Black College Republicans.
CHRIS
Drug addict. Auto mechanic. Ohio hair-do. Genius.
DAN
Theoretical manifestation of my best friend, who could be— but isn't—a punk.
FELICIA
Naïve, sexless West Coast denizen. Like the rest, she is doomed.
POPPY
On-and-off-again leader of formerly important nation.
THE GROUND RULES
• All characters may or may not appear in any situation under any identifier at the artist's discretion
• Then again, maybe not.
OUR GUARANTEE O' QUALITY
• All cartoons guaranteed drawn with genuine India ink!
• Very little humor lifted from Michael J. Fox films!
• Bob Hope, Elvis Presley and Garry Trudeau not used as primary influences!

YOUR CHECKLIST O' LOVE

BY TED RALL

IF YOU DON'T STOP COMING ON TO ME, I'LL TELL OUR BOSS.
IF YOU STILL DON'T STOP, I'LL CALL YOUR WIFE TO INFORM HER OF YOUR DISGUSTING BEHAVIOR.
AND IF THAT DOESN'T WORK, I'LL BREAK INTO YOUR HOUSE IN THE MIDDLE OF THE NIGHT, HEW OFF YOUR HEAD WITH A CARVING KNIFE AND BURY YOU IN A SHALLOW GRAVE.
FEISTY CHICKS DRIVE ME CRAZY.
TED RALL

GOOD MORNING, KEVIN, AND WELCOME TO LIFE. CONGRATULATIONS ON A SUCCESSFUL BIRTH WITHOUT DEFECTS OR COMPLICATIONS.
I HAVE BEEN APPOINTED BY YOUR PARENTS AS THEIR GUIDANCE ADVISOR IN RELATION TO THE MATTER OF YOUR UPBRINGING.
YOU WILL FIND IN FRONT OF YOU AN AGREEMENT DELINEATING YOUR PARENTS' RIGHTS AND RESPONSIBILITIES REGARDING YOUR MENTAL, EMOTIONAL AND PHYSICAL WELFARE OVER THE NEXT 40-TO-50 YEARS.
PURSUANT TO THE TERMS OF THIS RELATIONSHIP, YOUR PARENTS SHALL BE JOINT AND SEVERALLY LIABLE FOR ANY MISREPRESENTATIONS, GROSS NEGLIGENCE, BAD FAITH, ETC. YOU SHALL BE ENTITLED TO PERIODIC SUBSIDIES, TO WIT, PAYMENTS AND PARTIAL SUBSIDIES FOR FOOD, SHELTER, EDUCATIONAL PURPOSES, AND CLOTHING. PLEASE NOTE THE 2-AUTO LIMIT ON MAJOR ACCIDENTS IN YEARS 16 AND 17.
YOUR PARENTS SHALL BE AUTHORIZED TO MOLD YOUR SEXUAL AND POLITICAL ORIENTATION, YOUR SOCIOECONOMIC STATUS, MUSICAL PROCLIVITIES, NEUROSES, TRAUMAS, OPINIONS, FRIENDS, MATES, EATING HABITS, OUTERWARE, HOUSEKEEPING, EMPLOYMENT, RELATIONSHIPS, AND OTHER RELATED AND UNRELATED MATTERS, ALL AS SHALL BE SELECTED BY THEM IN THEIR SOLE DISCRETION UNLESS, OF COURSE, YOU ELECT THE ADOLESCENT RUNAWAY OPTION DURING PUBERTY.
I WOULD IN PARTICULAR CALL YOUR ATTENTION TO THE ABSENCE OF TERMINATION DATE. PLEASE SIGN CLEARLY ON BOTH COPIES.
©1990
TED RALL

NEW WAVE CAREERISM

YOUR DISCOUNT GUIDE TO AMERICAN RELIGION

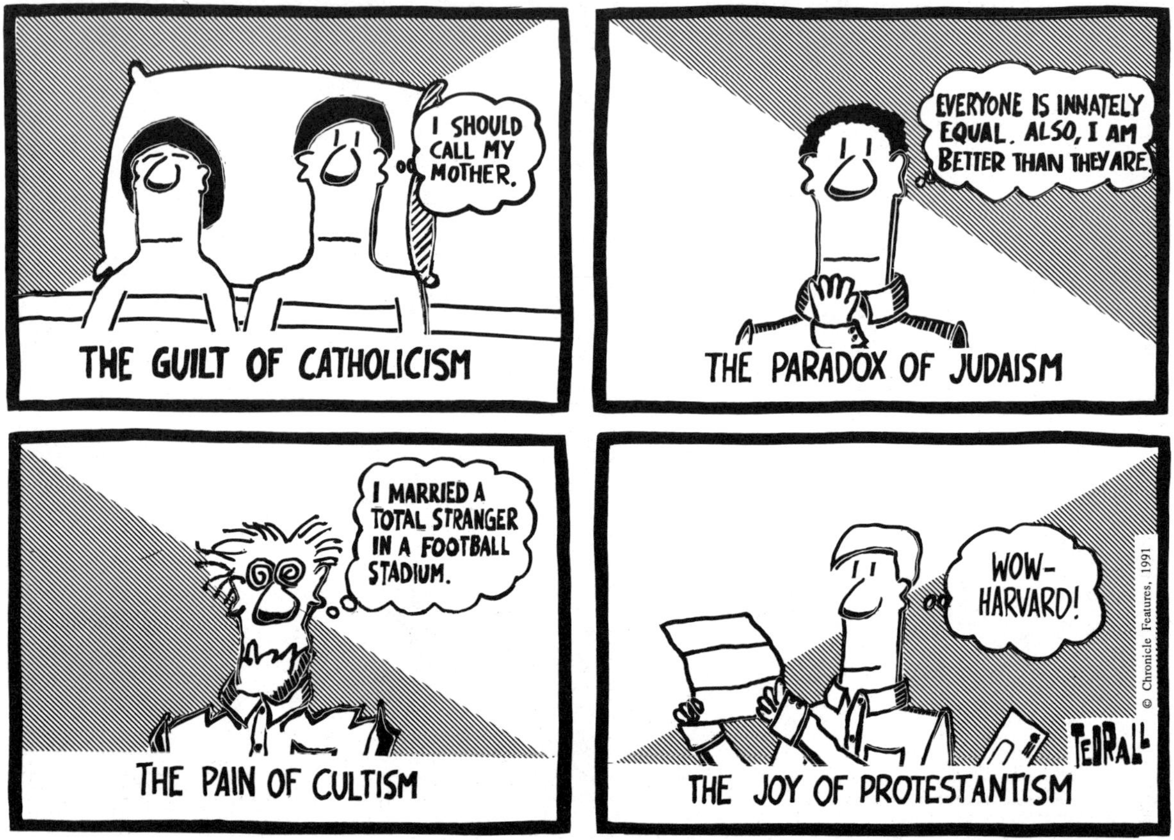

IT STARTED IN FLORIDA— HIGH SCHOOL KIDS LICKING POISONOUS TOADS FOR THEIR HALLUCINOGENIC SECRETIONS.*
THE TOAD WAR
*CARTOONIST'S GUARANTEE: THIS IS TRUE.
NOW THE TOAD SCOURGE IS EVERYWHERE. EVEN AS I SPEAK, YOUR KID COULD BE OUT SCORING SOME HIGH-POTENCY "GAINESVILLE GREEN"!
WALK
U.S.
F
SOME PEOPLE THINK INTERDICTION IS THE ANSWER, BUT THESE ANURAN NARCOTICS ARE IN EVERY POND—AND THEY'VE TURNED OUR INNER CITIES INTO A BATTLEGROUND. EDUCATION IS THE SOLUTION.
WHAT DRIVES A KID TO SEEK SOLACE FROM LIFE'S PROBLEMS IN THE GOOEY FLUIDS OF SOMETHING THAT EATS BUGS? BAD TASTE, MOSTLY. NOT TO MENTION BEING THE PRODUCT OF A BROKEN HOME.
BUT THESE ARE PROBLEMS WHICH WE HAVE NO DESIRE TO ADDRESS, EXCEPT TO GIVE YOU THIS FRIENDLY ADVICE: IF ANYONE OFFERS YOU A TEMPTING TOADY TREAT...
...JUST HOP AWAY.
©1990 TED RALL

WHEN LAYOFF VICTIMS BECOME DESPERATE
STAY AWAY FROM THE DESK! JUST ACT NORMALLY! WE'LL ALL PRETEND I STILL HAVE MY JOB... NOW BRING ME SOME FILES AND NOBODY WILL GET HURT!
ER CORP.
© Chronicle Features, 1992

YOUR CHECKLIST O' EMPLOYMENT by TED RALL
?
☐ A RAISE? YOU'RE LUCKY I DON'T KILL YOU!
☐ IT'S FOR YOUR OWN GOOD—WHAT WOULD YOU DO WITH ALL THAT MONEY?
☐ HA HA HA HA HA HA HA HA HA HA HA HA HA
☐ WE'RE STILL RECOVERING FROM TOUGH TIMES.
☐ WE'RE SUFFERING FROM TOUGH TIMES.
☐ WE'RE ANTICIPATING TOUGH TIMES.
☐ GEE, KID... I WAS JUST STARTING TO LIKE YOU!
☐ HUH? OH, I THOUGHT I HEARD SOMETHING, BUT I WAS WRONG.
☐ WHEN I WAS YOUR AGE...
☐ MONEY ISN'T EVERYTHING.
☐ I'M GLAD YOU BROUGHT THIS UP — NOW GET OUT.
☐ BUT YOU GOT A RAISE LAST YEAR!
☐ IF I'M NICE TO YOU NOW, YOU'LL LOSE YOUR MOTIVATION TO WORK.
☐ I APPRECIATE YOUR COURAGE IN COMING TO ME LIKE THIS. TELL ME: WERE YOU BORN STUPID OR DID YOUR MOM DROP YOU ON YOUR HEAD?
©1991

I WANT A JOB THAT I LIKE.
I WANT TO LOVE SOMEONE WHO LOVES ME.
I WANT AN APARTMENT BIG ENOUGH THAT I DON'T HAVE TO KEEP MY STUFF IN BOXES.
HERE - HAVE AN ESKIMO PIE.
TED RALL

EVER HAVE A SENSE OF IMPENDING DOOM?
NO.
ME NEITHER.
TED RALL

I LOVE YOU FOR THE FORSEEABLE FUTURE.
UNTIL SUCH TIME AS I FIND SOMEONE BETTER, I PLEDGE YOU MY UNDYING DEVOTION.
I MAY CHEAT ON YOU FROM TIME TO TIME, BUT SUCH ACTS OF INFIDELITY SHALL OCCUR ONLY FOR SEXUAL LIAISONS WITH ONLY MINIMAL IMPACT ON OUR RELATIONSHIP.
WE SHALL TAKE ALL NECESSARY BIRTH CONTROL PRECAUTIONS TO ENSURE THAT WE SHALL NOT CREATE ANY POTENTIAL OFFSPRING TO BE ABUSED.
IF AT ANY TIME YOU SHOULD DETERMINE IN YOUR SOLE DISCRETION THAT OUR RELATION-SHIP IS NOT FEASIBLE, WE SHALL ENTER INTO NEGOTIATIONS TO DIVIDE OUR OFFSPRING AND OTHER COMMUNAL PROPERTY.
PLEASE NOTE THAT THIS AGREEMENT WILL CEASE UPON DEATH, MENTAL INSTABILITY OR BOTH.

I GOT NOTHIN' TO DO. I GOT NO PROSPECTS. AND I GOT NO HOPE.
BEING LAID OFF MEANS NO PLANS. NO PURCHASES. NO SOCIAL LIFE. NO ENTERTAINMENT. NOTHING.
ALL I HAVE IS TIME TO WASTE, PLUS NOTHING TO LOSE.
© 1991 TED RALL
I HEREBY DECLARE MY INTENTION TO SEEK THE DEMOCRATIC NOMINATION FOR THE PRESIDENCY.

WE HAVE EVIDENCE THAT REAGAN AND BUSH CONSPIRED WITH IRAN TO DELAY THE HOSTAGE RELEASE TO STEAL THE 1980 ELECTION!
SO WHAT?
A REPORTER INVESTIGATING THE "OCTOBER SURPRISE" WAS FOUND DEAD. THE COPS SAY IT'S SUICIDE, BUT THE EVIDENCE POINTS TO MURDER!
WHERE'S THE STORY?
BOTH OLLIE NORTH AND FORMER IRANIAN PRESIDENT BANI-SADR SAY REAGAN KNEW ABOUT AND ORDERED THE WHOLE THING!
BOR-RING!
MADONNA, CHER AND AXL ROSE LAUNDERED THE CASH AND PERFORMED LEWD ACTS WITH THE AYATOLLAH IN PARIS IN OCTOBER 1980!
STOP THE PRESSES!
TEDRALL

AMERICAN DREAMS FOR THE '90s

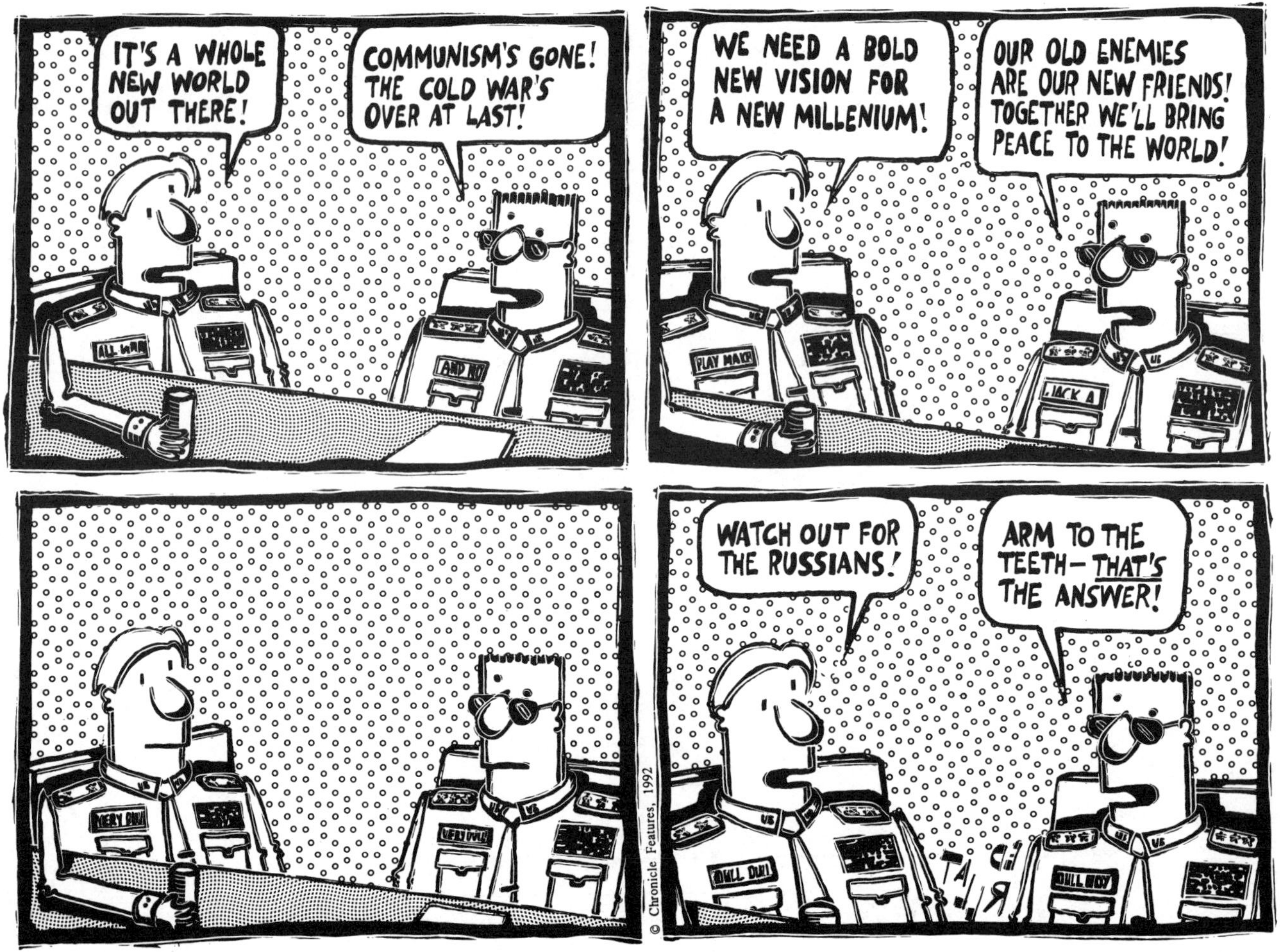
IT'S A WHOLE NEW WORLD OUT THERE!
COMMUNISM'S GONE! THE COLD WAR'S OVER AT LAST!
WE NEED A BOLD NEW VISION FOR A NEW MILLENIUM!
OUR OLD ENEMIES ARE OUR NEW FRIENDS! TOGETHER WE'LL BRING PEACE TO THE WORLD!
WATCH OUT FOR THE RUSSIANS!
ARM TO THE TEETH—THAT'S THE ANSWER!

LIFE IN POST-THOMAS AMERICA

IT'S TOUGH TO BE A WHITE MALE THESE DAYS...
YOU'RE AUTOMATICALLY ASSUMED TO BE A POTENTIAL RAPIST OR CLOSET KLANSMAN...
YOU HAVE TO ACCEPT THE BLAME FOR VIOLENCE AND EXPLOITATION YOU HAD NOTHING TO DO WITH...
AND WHEN YOU TRY TO HELP WOMEN AND MINORITIES, YOU'RE CONSIDERED PATRONIZING.
SOMETIMES IT MAKES ME WANT TO KILL THEM ALL.
© 1991 TED RALL

THE FIRST HONEST CANDIDATE.

I SUPPOSE IT WAS INEVITABLE, BUT IT'S STILL KINDA WEIRD.
I'LL NEED THAT MEMO BEFORE YOU GO HOME TONIGHT, OK?
NIRVANA
DURING AN ERA OF DIMINISHED EXPECTATIONS, PEOPLE SEEK OUT VICARIOUS PLEASURES TO REPLACE REAL ONES.
THE PROMOTION'S GOING TO DAVE. SORRY. MAYBE NEXT YEAR.
DRAMARAMA
WE BUY VIDEOS THAT SHOW THE OCEAN, FOREIGN CITIES, FIREPLACES AND PASTURES—RATHER THAN SEE THEM FOR REAL.
I KNOW IT'S A HOLIDAY WEEKEND, BUT WE NEED YOU TO FLY TO DAYTON.
BUZZCOCKS
I DON'T CARE WHAT YOU THINK... I LOVE MY EMPLOYMENT VIDEO!
THE EFFECT WOULD BE BETTER IF YOU'D SHUT OFF THE VENTILATION AND INSTALL FLUORESCENT LIGHTING...
SHAPE UP OR YOU'RE FIRED!
TED RALL

BACK IN COLLEGE, I GOT DISGUSTED BY THE OTHER STUDENTS. ALL THEY WANTED WAS TO GET A JOB THAT PAID A LOT OF MONEY. SO I DROPPED OUT.
THEN I GOT A JOB. I GOT DISGUSTED WITH MY COWORKERS. ALL THEY CARED ABOUT WAS MAKING MORE MONEY. SO I QUIT.
I DECIDED TO BECOME AN ALL-PURPOSE WRITER/POET/PUNK MUSICIAN/POLITICAL ACTIVIST. BUT THAT STUFF WAS ALL ABOUT MONEY, TOO. SO I GOT DISILLUSIONED. NOW I JUST HANG OUT.
HERE'S YOUR CAPPUCINO. THAT'LL BE THREE BUCKS.
TED RALL

FUN WITH CONTRACEPTION
I WOULD LIKE TO TAKE THIS OPPORTUNITY TO ASSURE YOU THAT I NOT ONLY WEAR VERY TIGHT UNDERWEAR—I ALSO DOWNED 12 BEERS DURING THE LAST 2 HOURS, THEREBY RADICALLY REDUCING MY SPERM PRODUCTION!
ALSO, I LOVE YOU!
AS FOR ME, I'M A DILIGENT SMOKER... AT 3 PACKS A DAY, MY FERTILITY IS HISTORY!
ALSO, I LOVE YOU TOO!
TEDRALL
© Chronicle Features, 1991

MODERN PHOBIAS
BY TED RALL © 1990
FURTIMFURIOSIAMATOSOMNIDISVISCEROPHOBIA:
THE FEAR THAT YOUR LOVER IS SECRETLY PLOTTING TO DISEMBOWEL YOU WHILE YOU'RE ASLEEP
SKI
EFFECTUSVIRIDIDOMOPHOBIA:
THE FEAR THAT IT WILL NEVER SNOW AGAIN
MEDIUMSACCOPHOBIA:
THE FEAR OF PEOPLE WHO WEAR BLACK WAIST POUCHES
SUMPTUOSISORDOSINEOPUSOPHOBIA:
THE FEAR OF NOT LANDING A JOB AFTER SPENDING $80,000 ON A COLLEGE DEGREE

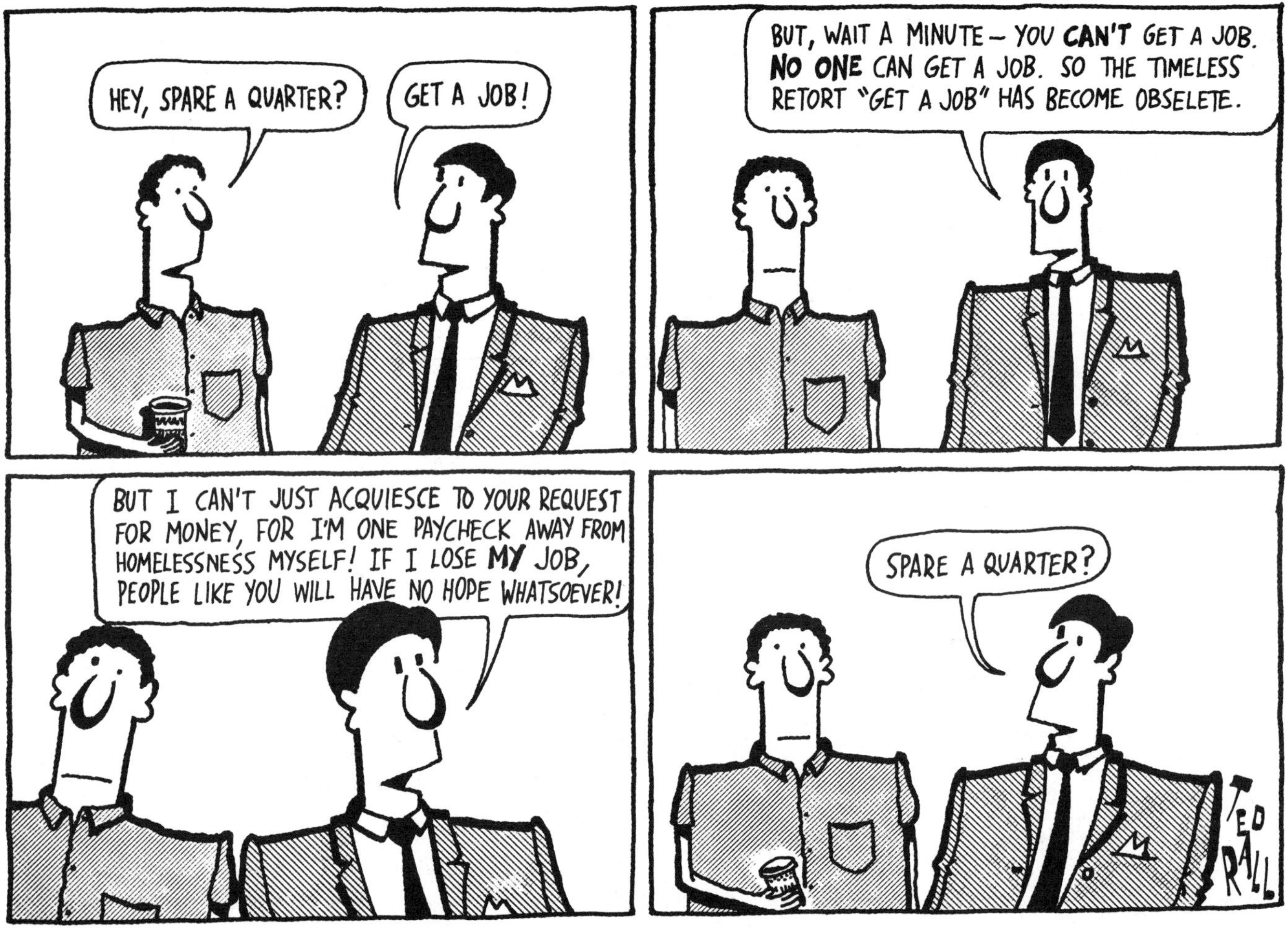
HEY, SPARE A QUARTER?
GET A JOB!
BUT, WAIT A MINUTE – YOU **CAN'T** GET A JOB. **NO ONE** CAN GET A JOB. SO THE TIMELESS RETORT "GET A JOB" HAS BECOME OBSELETE.
BUT I CAN'T JUST ACQUIESCE TO YOUR REQUEST FOR MONEY, FOR I'M ONE PAYCHECK AWAY FROM HOMELESSNESS MYSELF! IF I LOSE **MY** JOB, PEOPLE LIKE YOU WILL HAVE NO HOPE WHATSOEVER!
SPARE A QUARTER?
TED RALL

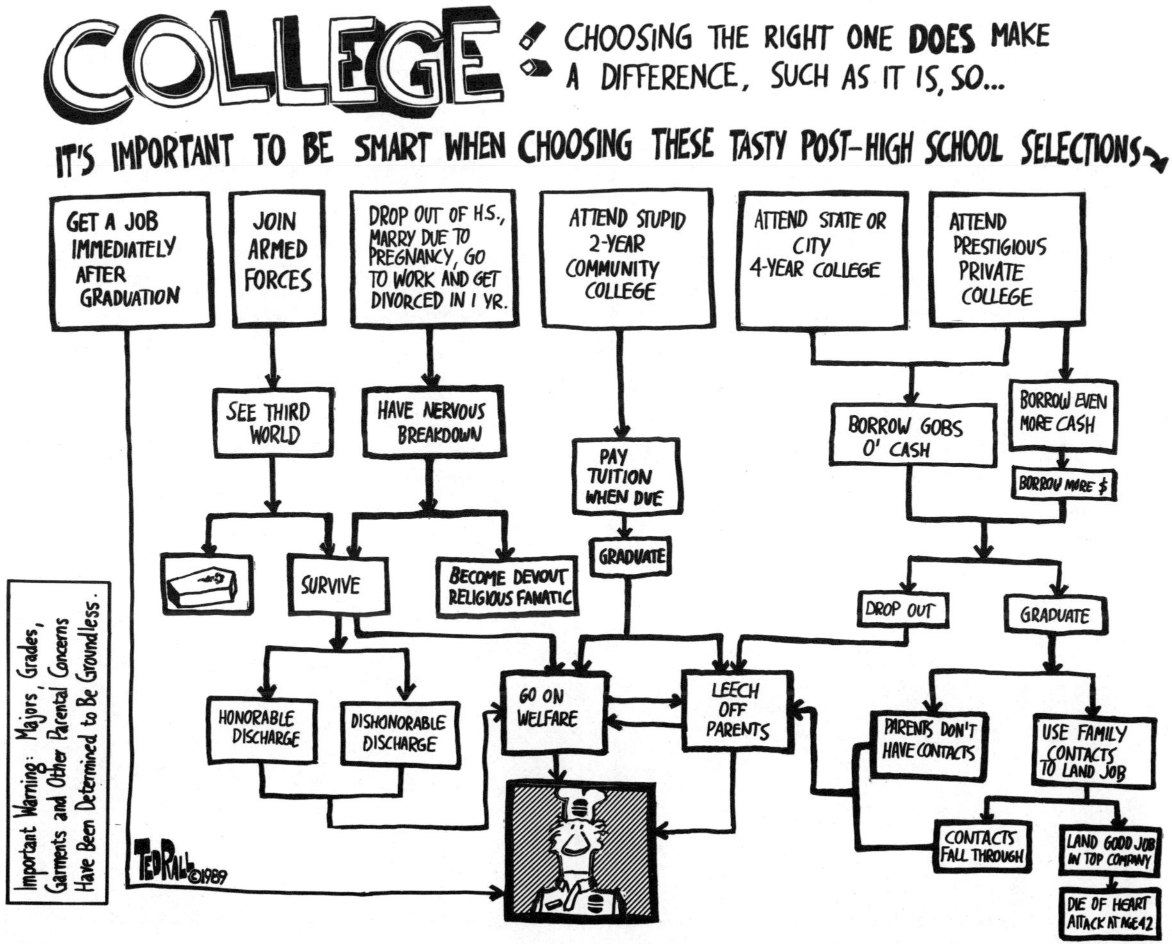
COLLEGE: CHOOSING THE RIGHT ONE DOES MAKE A DIFFERENCE, SUCH AS IT IS, SO...
IT'S IMPORTANT TO BE SMART WHEN CHOOSING THESE TASTY POST-HIGH SCHOOL SELECTIONS
GET A JOB IMMEDIATELY AFTER GRADUATION
JOIN ARMED FORCES
DROP OUT OF H.S., MARRY DUE TO PREGNANCY, GO TO WORK AND GET DIVORCED IN 1 YR.
ATTEND STUPID 2-YEAR COMMUNITY COLLEGE
ATTEND STATE OR CITY 4-YEAR COLLEGE
ATTEND PRESTIGIOUS PRIVATE COLLEGE
SEE THIRD WORLD
HAVE NERVOUS BREAKDOWN
PAY TUITION WHEN DUE
BORROW GOBS O' CASH
BORROW EVEN MORE CASH
BORROW MORE $
SURVIVE
BECOME DEVOUT RELIGIOUS FANATIC
GRADUATE
DROP OUT
GRADUATE
HONORABLE DISCHARGE
DISHONORABLE DISCHARGE
GO ON WELFARE
LEECH OFF PARENTS
PARENTS DON'T HAVE CONTACTS
USE FAMILY CONTACTS TO LAND JOB
CONTACTS FALL THROUGH
LAND GOOD JOB IN TOP COMPANY
DIE OF HEART ATTACK AT AGE 42
Important Warning: Majors, Grades, Garments and Other Parental Concerns Have Been Determined to Be Groundless.
TED RALL ©1989

DERISIVE REMARK
SNOTTY REPLY
HOME SWEET ETC.
IRATE PARENTAL REPRIMAND, DEMAND FOR RETRACTION UNDER VAGUE THREAT OF PUNISHMENT
REBELLIOUS DECLARATION OF AUTONOMY
GOD BLESS THIS GENERIC HOUSE
REMINDER OF FINANCIAL CONTROL
GRUDGING ACKNOWLEDGEMENT OF SUBSERVIENCE; APOLOGY FOLLOWED BY PROFESSION OF SHOCK AT UNFAIRNESS OF EXISTING ORDER OF THINGS
HOME IS WHERE THE RADON IS
DERISIVE REMARK
LOVE YOUR SUBURB
TED RALL
©1990

FUN WITH UNDEREMPLOYMENT
SURE, THE PAY COULD BE BETTER. AND THE WORK COULD BE MORE INTERESTING. AND MY COWORKERS...WHAT A BUNCH OF STIFFS! OBVIOUSLY, THIS JOB IS MILES BENEATH ME. ON THE OTHER HAND, IT'S NOT TOO DEMANDING AND IT COULD BE WORSE—A LOT OF PEOPLE HAVE NO JOB AT ALL!
© Chronicle Features, 1991
TED RALL

YOUR E-Z GUIDE TO 90's WOMANHOOD

SOVIET HISTORY AT A GLANCE
CZARIST RUSSIA
ONLY THE RICH HAVE FOOD.
EARLY COMMUNISM
NOBODY HAS ANY FOOD. WE ALL SHARE IT EQUALLY.
LATE COMMUNISM
ONLY THE PRIVILEGED HAVE DECENT FOOD.
CAPITALISM
I CAN SEE FOOD ON TV!
©1991 CHRONICLE FEATURES
TED RALL
© Chronicle Features, 1991

SMOKING: NOT JUST A HABIT.
I WAS WORRIED TO DEATH THAT MY CHILDREN WOULD NEVER BE ABLE TO AFFORD COLLEGE.
THEN I READ AN ARTICLE ABOUT A NEW JERSEY WOMAN WHO WON $400,000 FROM A TOBACCO COMPANY AFTER SHE DIED OF CANCER.
SO I WORKED OUT MY COURSE OF ACTION... SHE SMOKED 2 PACKS A DAY FOR 40 YEARS—A TOTAL OF 584,000 CIGARETTES. THAT'S 68¢ EACH.
I STARTED SMOKING YESTERDAY. I GO THROUGH 12 PACKS A DAY! I FIGURE I'LL BE A MILLIONAIRE IN 17 YEARS... BETTER THAN ANY PENSION!
BESIDES, IT'LL BE HARVARD FOR MY KIDS!
I LOVE MY FAMILY. THAT'S WHY I SMOKE.
HIS
CIGS
UNFILTERED STINKY BUTTS
HERS
Smokettes
DAINTY PHALLIC MENTHOL FILTERED
SMOKING.
IT'S AN INVESTMENT.

THE STATISTICS OF LOVE
LET'S ASSUME THERE IS SOMEBODY FOR EVERYBODY AND THAT PERSON IS OUT THERE SOMEWHERE WAITING FOR YOU.
WHAT ARE THE ODDS OF THAT PERSON BEING OF THE RIGHT SEX? THE RIGHT SEXUAL ORIENTATION? THE RIGHT NATIONALITY, RELIGION AND SOCIOECONOMIC STATUS? OF BEING SINGLE OR WILLING TO BECOME SINGLE?
NEWS
WHAT ARE THE CHANCES OF THAT SPECIAL PERSON MEETING YOU? OF LIKING YOU? OF LIKING YOU AT THE SAME TIME YOU LIKE HIM OR HER? OF GETTING MARRIED?
ARE YOU TRYING TO TELL ME SOMETHING?
NO, NOTHING.
TED RALL

GOOD MORNING, SUNBEAM!
(SNIFF SNIFF) WHAT THE...?
I STILL SAY THE GREENHOUSE EFFECT REQUIRES MORE STUDY.
APOLOGIES TO CHANCE BROWN AND GREG & BRIAN WALKER
TED RALL

WHY GUN CONTROL IS A GOOD IDEA.

HOW POSTAL CLERKS GET RAISES

CF 121691-A

I CAN'T BELIEVE IT! AFTER 20 YEARS ON THE JOB, ALL I GET IS TWO WEEKS SEVERANCE AND "SEE YA AROUND"!
SO WHAT ARE YOU PLANNING TO DO?
FRANKLY, I WAS THINKING ALONG THE LINES OF A MASS MURDER-SUICIDE...
WHAT WOULD THAT SOLVE? YOU HAVE TO STOP BLAMING YOUR BOSS!
DON'T BE SUCH A FOOL! NO ONE OWES YOU A JOB! FORGET LIFETIME EMPLOYMENT! SEIZE THIS OPPORTUNITY-- GET JOB TRAINING AND TURN YOUR WHOLE LIFE AROUND!
YOU'RE RIGHT! I'LL TAKE SOME ACCOUNTING CLASSES SO I CAN EMBEZZLE FROM MY NEXT EMPLOYER!
NOW YOU'RE TALKING LIKE A REAL AMERICAN!
TED RALL

TIRED OF WORKING FOR MINIMUM WAGE?
WHY NOT CONSIDER A CAREER AS A
U.S. CONGRESSMAN?
Are you:
WHITE?
MALE?
WEALTHY?
MIDDLE-AGED?
If so, you too can enjoy:
• GUARANTEED PAY INCREASES
• OCCASIONAL WHITE HOUSE DINNERS
• LIASONS WITH ATTRACTIVE PAGES
• ENDLESS OPPORTUNITIES FOR EXTRA INCOME
• EVERYONE ELSE EARNING 1981 WAGES
• LIVING AWAY FROM YOUR DUMPY DISTRICT
CLIP 'N' SEND
YES! I WANT MORE INFORMATION ON HOW I CAN BECOME AN OFFICIAL U.S. CONGRESSMAN! I UNDERSTAND THAT THERE'S NO RISK OF HAVING TO TAKE ANY ACTION WHATSOEVER! RUSH ME A STACK OF BALLOT PETITIONS, PRONTO!
I'M: ☐ WHITE ☐ MALE ☐ ET CETERA
NAME
ADDRESS
CITY STATE ZIP
SEND TO: House of Representatives
P.O. Box SP-1989
Washington, D.C. 20515
Attention: Special Offer Section
"AT $135,000 A YEAR, WE CONGRESSPEOPLE ARE JUST SCRAPING BY. BUT, HEY—THERE'S ALWAYS NEXT YEAR!" – Generic Congressman
TED RALL ©1989

SAY, MIKE – YOU'RE IN THE C.I.A... THE COLD WAR'S OVER... HOW 'BOUT 'FESSING UP ABOUT WHO KILLED KENNEDY?
LEE HARVEY OSWALD ACTED ALONE.
JAMES EARL RAY ACTED ALONE.
SO DID SIRHAN SIRHAN, SQUEAKY FROMME AND JOHN HINCKLEY. AND IF YOU DON'T BELIEVE ME...
SO WILL WE.
TED RALL

BERLIN, 1945.
GENTLEMEN, WE ARE HERE FOR ONE PURPOSE - TO PREPARE A NATIONAL SOCIALIST FUTURE WITHOUT GERMANY. HAVE MY ORDERS BEEN COMPLIED WITH?
MEIN FÜHRER, PLAN "AMERIKA 90" IS IN FULL EFFECT. WE HAVE PLACED SPECIALLY TRAINED AGENTS THROUGHOUT AMERICA'S GOVERNMENT AND INDUSTRY. WITH THE BENEFITS OF SUPERB PLASTIC SURGERY, FORGED DOCUMENTS AND PERFECT POSITIONING, THEY WILL CERTAINLY SUCCEED WHERE WE HAVE FAILED!
OUR MEN WILL PROMOTE AN IMPERIALIST, ANTI-COMMUNIST FOREIGN POLICY WHICH WILL CULMINATE IN ENORMOUS EXPENDITURES ON ARMS. IT SHOULD REQUIRE ABOUT 40 YEARS FOR THE U.S. ECONOMY TO COLLAPSE ENTIRELY!
SOON YOUNG AMERICANS WILL FIND THAT THEY WON'T BE ABLE TO BUY CARS OR HOUSES; THEY'LL BE MURDERED BY HIGH TAXES AT THEIR MEDIOCRE, LOW-PAYING JOBS. THEY'LL BE LOOKING FOR SIMPLE, FAST SOLUTIONS... SOLUTIONS ONLY ONE POLITICAL PARTY CAN PROVIDE!
A.H.
ONCE THE POLITICAL AND ECONOMIC CLIMATES ARE DOMINATED BY DISTRUST AND DISINTEGRATION, YOU WILL RETURN FROM EXILE AS A CAB DRIVER IN BELIZE! THE REICH WILL RISE AGAIN FROM THE WHITE HOUSE!
OF COURSE, THE PLAN ASSUMES THAT THE AMERICANS WILL ONLY ELECT PRESIDENTS AND CONGRESSMEN WHO ARE SPINELESS, SNIVELING, FACELESS OPPORTUNISTIC HACKS.
THAT IS A LOT TO HOPE FOR, MEIN FÜHRER.
©1990 TED RALL
NEXT: WHY YOU SHOULD NEVER, EVER PAY ATTENTION TO WEIRD CONSPIRACY THEORIES

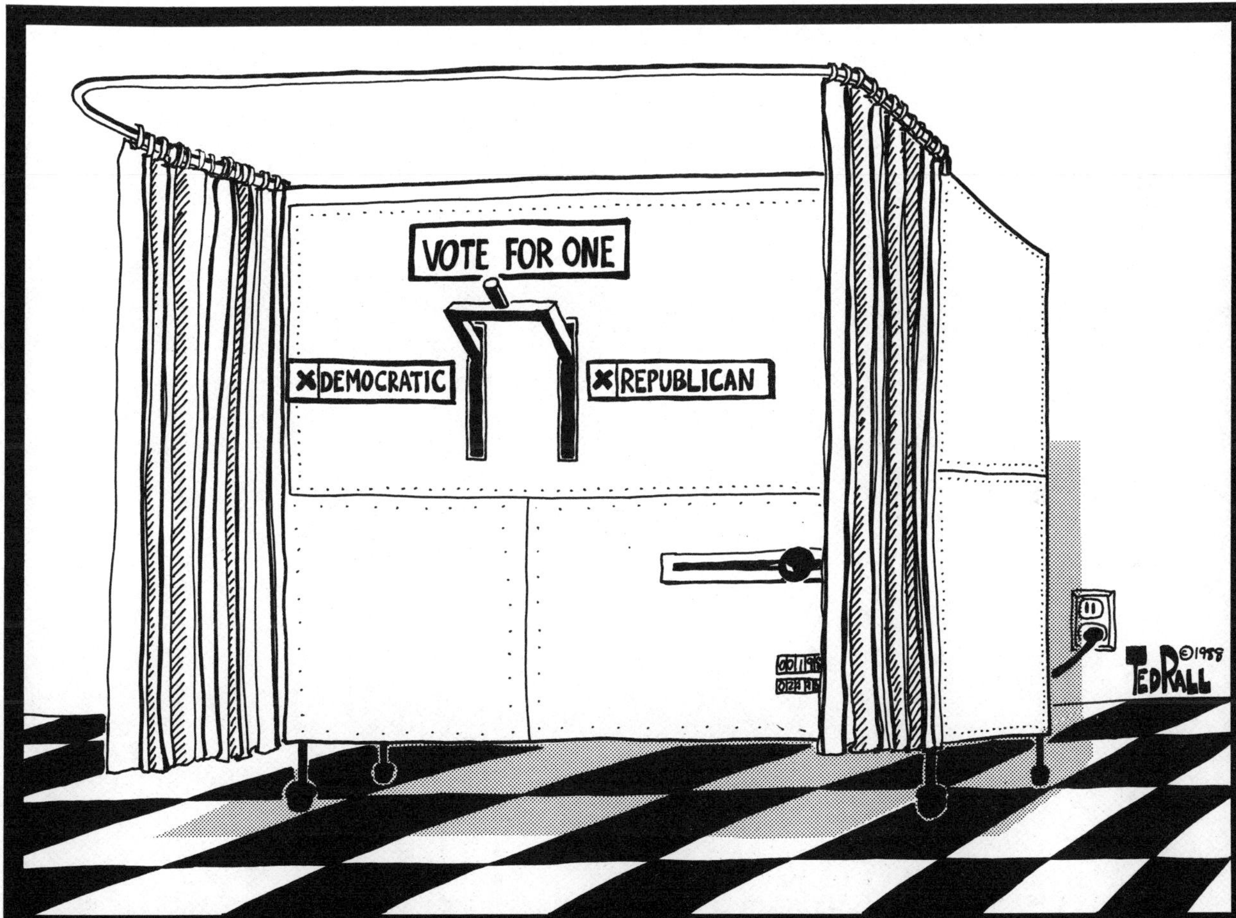
VOTE FOR ONE
DEMOCRATIC
REPUBLICAN
©1988
TED RALL

AMERICANS ARE SO STRANGE.
THEY ALWAYS WANT ONE SEAT LEFT EMPTY ON EACH SIDE OF THEM, EXCEPT FOR THE PEOPLE THEY CAME WITH...
SO LATECOMERS CAN'T SIT TOGETHER, BECAUSE ONLY SINGLE SEATS ARE LEFT.
© TED RALL 1991
DON'T TOUCH ME

HOW PRO-CHOICERS ARE BORN
© Chronicle Features, 1991
?
OOPS.
TED RALL

ONE DAY, JUST LIKE USUAL, DAVE'S ALARM CLOCK RANG. HE GOT UP AND LOOKED OUTSIDE.
7:15
AT FIRST, IT LOOKED LIKE ANY OTHER DAY.
BUT THERE WAS SOMETHING VERY DIFFERENT IN THE AIR.
AT FIRST, DAVE WAS CONFUSED.
LATER, HE FELT FLATTERED.
BUT, DAY AFTER DAY, WHAT WAS ONCE VERY SURPRISING BECAME VERY ORDINARY.
SOUTH FERRY
LOCAL
LIFE WENT BY EVERY DAY PRETTY MUCH AS IT ALWAYS HAD, EXCEPT FOR DAVE'S PERSONALITY CULT.
BUS
DAVE ATE A LOT. HE BOUGHT A LOT OF CLOTHES. HE GOT PARANOID. HE STOPPED RETURNING CALLS.
ONE DAY, THEY CAME AND SHOT DAVE.
TED RALL ©1990

I HAVE THE SAME CHANCES AS ANYONE ELSE, AS LONG AS THEY'RE ON MY SOCIO-ECONOMIC LEVEL.
OFFICE OF FINANCIAL AID
I HAVE THE RIGHT OF PRIVACY WHEN I BUY CIGARETTES, BUT NOT WHEN I BUY RUBBERS.
CONDOMS
FOR ALL
SMOKE!
Cigarettes
WHEN I GO TO THE MOVIES, I'M AN ADULT; WHEN I'M IN SCHOOL, I'M LESS THAN HUMAN.
THE OOZE
ADULTS
CHILDREN
(UNDER 12)
I'M ENTITLED TO A TRIAL BY A JURY OF MY PEERS, ALTHOUGH MY PEERS CAN'T BE JURORS.
6'
5'
POLICE
3742420
WHEN I TURN 18, I'LL BE ABLE TO VOTE AND BE DRAFTED, THOUGH UNABLE TO DRINK OR RUN FOR OFFICE.
ANOTHER 7-UP OVER HERE...
ARMY
AMERICA'S YOUTH — NOW AVAILABLE AS HANDY DISPOSABLES.
TedRall

I'VE BEEN THINKING TOO MUCH LATELY...
...PERHAPS SOME TV?
2 TV Movie "Despair." Meryl Streep stars as a welfare mother who murders her newborn son in the fitting room of a department store to keep her food stamps.
SEX ON TV: Full Color Photo Analysis
TV GUIDE
These Commie Newscasters PAGE 17
4 Docudrama "The Death of Julia." Parents cope with their daughter's terminal anorexia.
AL'S BOOZE
7 9 Special Report "Pain in America." News crews interview the homeless in New York, the poor in Appalachia, women who get abortions in Canada due to a lack of insurance.
Christian TV:
©1989 TedRall
11 Analysis "Gaza." Israeli settlers and Palestinian refuges discover peace by shooting holes through each other. Narrated by Kris Kristoff and George C. Scott.
Smoke Now
TV: Why Is It So Stupid?
THANK GOD FOR PUBLIC TELEVISION!
TONIGHT, ON "MASTERPIECE THEATRE": "FLAMING BOSOMS, PART 7."
KLIK

POST MODERN AMBITION
by TED RALL
WITH MY DOCTORATE IN BEHAVIORAL PSYCHOLOGY, I'M A CINCH FOR THAT DAY-CARE JOB!
ONCE THE BOSS HEARS MY PLAN TO SAVE GOBS OF CASH ON MY PENSION BY KILLING MYSELF, I'LL DEFINITELY KEEP MY JOB... MAYBE.
I'M GOING TO SCORE A DREARY MENIAL JOB TO PAY THE RENT WHILE I WORK FOR FREE IN THE FIELD OF MY CHOICE!
Miller
©1991

IT'S DINNER UNDER THE STARS EVERY NIGHT WHEN YOU'RE
HOMELESS!
GET ALL THE FACTS
CHECK OUT THESE BENEFITS TODAY:
TED RALL ©1990
I'M A HAPPY CAMPER
FREE RENT
NO BORING JOB
ADVENTURE GALORE
SANITY OPTIONAL
NO MORE SHAVING
Paint Thinner
EXCITING NEW BEVERAGES
AGE 4 PLEASE HELP
NO EXPERIENCE NECESSARY
Do you have what it takes to become homeless?
HEAD
ARMS
LEGS
HOMELESSNESS IS PATRIOTIC!
When you "go homeless," you:
• FREE UP VALUABLE REAL ESTATE & JOBS!
• MAKE THE MIDDLE CLASS FEEL THAT THEY'RE BETTER OFF THAN YOU!
• DISAPPEAR FROM THE WORK FORCE – AND REDUCE UNEMPLOYMENT!
• ELIMINATE OVERPOPULATION BY CENSUS OVERSIGHT!
CLIP 'N' SEND TO LANDLORD, EMPLOYER & PARENTS:
Date: ________
Dear Sir or Madam:
I hereby withdraw from life, you repulsive scum.
Your tenant/minion/etc.,
____
JOIN AMERICA'S FASTEST GROWING DEMOGRAPHIC GROUP!
The City of New York
NYC Department of Sanitation
Bureau of Waste Disposal
137 Centre Street, Rm 104
New York, NY 10013
Equal Opportunity Employer

Don't just talk about the down and out – hang out with them!
TAKE MASS TRANSIT TODAY!
TIRED OF TRAFFIC? PARKING HASSLES? RISING GAS PRICES? TRADE IN YOUR CAR KEYS FOR A $150 MONTHLY COMMUTER PASS AND A GREASY SEAT ON ONE OF THESE ENVIRONMENTALLY-CORRECT TRANSPORTATION ALTERNATIVES:
SUBWAY
BUS
COMMUTER RAIL
• EXPERIENCE INTERACTION WITH HOSTILE YOUTHS
• TRAVEL IN THE COMFORT OF A SMALL METAL BOX HURTLING THROUGH A DARK TUNNEL WITHOUT OXYGEN
• STOPS OFTEN
• STOPS SOME MORE
• STOPS AGAIN
• COMES NOW AND THEN, TOO
• LEAVES FROM STATION CONVENIENTLY WITHIN DRIVING DISTANCE OF HOME
• HARDLY EVER DERAILS AT 60+ MPH
• YOUR CAR MAY BE THERE WHEN YOU GET HOME
TED RALL

YOU HAVE A CHOICE: WE CAN CUT YOUR SALARY, YANK YOUR UNION CARD, ELIMINATE YOUR HEALTH INSURANCE, PENSION AND PROFIT SHARING AND DEMOTE YOU.
OR WE CAN FIRE YOU AND YOU CAN LAND A JOB SOMEWHERE ELSE AT LOWER PAY, WITHOUT A UNION OR BENEFITS. WE'LL JUST REPLACE YOU WITH SOMEONE WHO GOT FIRED BY SOMEONE ELSE. IT'S UP TO YOU. LET ME KNOW WHAT YOU DECIDE.
JUST KIDDING.
TED RALL

REAL LIFE COMICS
"YOU KNOW IT'S REAL LIFE WHEN THE PUNCH LINE IS ALWAYS THE SAME"
STEVE LIVED IN HIS DIRTY, CRAMPED APARTMENT
HE WORKED NEARBY AT HIS BORING, HOPELESS JOB
WHERE HE MET A WOMAN WHO TOLD HIM THAT SHE LOVED HIM
ATTENTION EMPLOYEES: DO NOT HANG OUT BY THE WATER COOLER!
!
HE MARRIED HER, BOUGHT A HOUSE AND RAISED TWO KIDS WHO NEVER CALLED
HOME SWEET SOMETHING
SHE LEFT, HE RETIRED AND WATCHED TV IN HIS TIDY, EMPTY HOUSE
ONE MORNING, HE WOKE UP DEAD.
©1990 TED RALL

YOUR PROBLEM IS THAT YOU'RE TOO NEGATIVE.
YOUR DEPRESSION MAKES YOU ANGRY AND ANTAGONISTIC, SO YOUR CO-WORKERS REACT ACCORDINGLY AND YOUR PESSIMISM BECOMES JUSTIFIED.
YOUR BAD ATTITUDE IS A SELF-FULFILLING PROPHECY; YOU CREATE YOUR OWN REALITY.
SHAPE UP OR YOU'RE FIRED.
TODD RALL

EARLY WARNING SIGNS: INCOMPATIBILITY

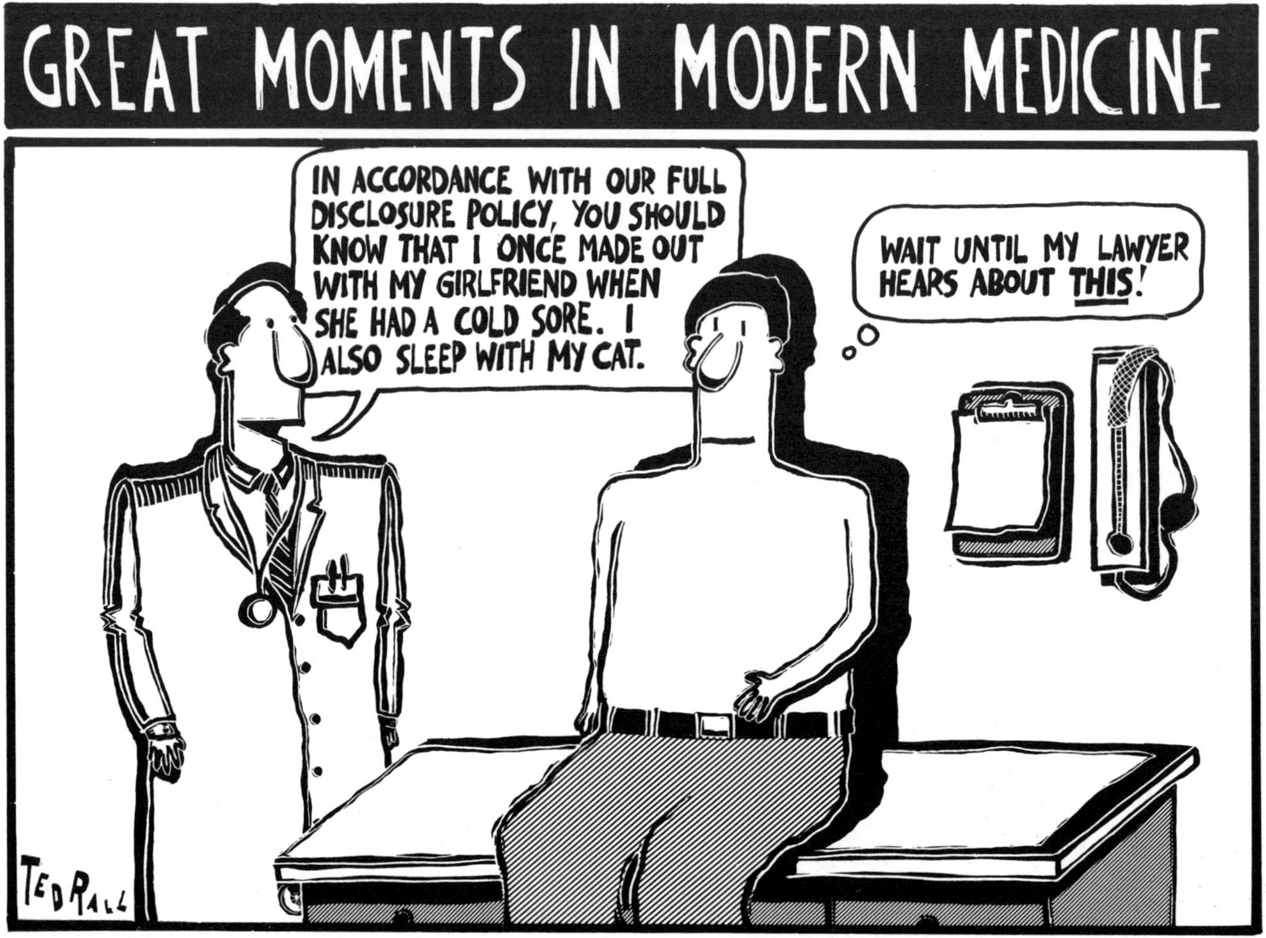
GREAT MOMENTS IN MODERN MEDICINE
IN ACCORDANCE WITH OUR FULL DISCLOSURE POLICY, YOU SHOULD KNOW THAT I ONCE MADE OUT WITH MY GIRLFRIEND WHEN SHE HAD A COLD SORE. I ALSO SLEEP WITH MY CAT.
WAIT UNTIL MY LAWYER HEARS ABOUT THIS!
TED RALL

POST-FEMINIST CHIVALRY
BY TED RALL ©1991
HAVING BEEN SUBJUGATED, HUMILIATED, EXPLOITED, ABUSED, RAPED, ENSLAVED AND SYSTEMATICALLY OPPRESSED FOR MILLIONS OF YEARS, YOU, AS A REPRESENTATIVE OF THE FEMALE GENDER, MUST BE EXHAUSTED. ACCORDINGLY, THE LEAST THAT I, A MEMBER OF A VIOLENT, BRUTAL SEX, CAN DO IS TO HOLD THIS DOOR OPEN FOR YOU!
WASTE

"★★★★ STYLISH AND VISUALLY SPLENDID..."
– BAYONNE ADVERTISER
"...visionary ...stylish."
– INSECT WORLD
"See it for the typeset alone... nobody knows what it's about... important."
– BATHROOM GRAFFITI
A MOVIE WITH
ART DECO LOGO
PRETENSE FILMS PRESENT A CHET AND VIRGIL PRODUCTION STARRING ABSOLUTELY NO ONE
YOU'VE EVER, EVER, EVEN REMOTELY HEARD OF AND HIS AND/OR HER NEXTDOOR NEIGHBOR'S CAT
IN A MOVIE WITH ART DECO LOGO MUSIC BY TANGERINE DREAM WRITTEN BY F. SCOTT FITZGERALD'S GRANDSON'S TAILOR
©1990
TED RALL

"HANDY" HOUSEHOLD HINT #9 by TED RALL
I'LL NEVER BE ABLE TO AFFORD A DISHWASHER ON A BEEKEEPER'S SALARY! IT'S SO DEPRESSING... I'M DOOMED TO POVERTY AND DISHPAN HANDS!!
$775 SALE
EAT THE RICH
THAT'S NOT TRUE! EVERYBODY ALREADY HAS A DISHWASHER!!!
SIMPLY FOLLOW THESE EASY INSTRUCTIONS:
APPROVED
FAST
HOUSEKEEPING
1 GATHER DIRTY DISHES.
ROLLING ROCK
2 OPEN LID; ADD CLEANSER.
3 PLACE COLLANDER AT BOTTOM OF BOWL AND ADD DIRTY DISHES.
4 FLUSH 5 TIMES VIGOROUSLY.
5 REMOVE AND DRY DISHES.
PRESTO — THEY'RE VIRTUALLY IMMACULATE!
COMING SOON:
The Quick, Easy Way to Do Your Laundry...without Appliances!

HI! DO YOU HAVE THE TIME?
WHAT KIND OF RACIST ARE YOU?
EXCUSE ME?
ARE YOU AN OLD-FASHIONED RACIST, WHO SEEKS OUT MINORITY WOMEN TO SUBJUGATE THEM AND EXPRESS MALE DOMINANCE? IF SO, YOU CAN COUNT ME OUT!
OR ARE YOU A POLITICALLY-CORRECT RACIST WHO WANTS TO ADD MULTICULTURAL NOTCHES TO HIS BEDPOST? MAYBE YOU'RE AN INSECURE RACIST WHO'S AFRAID TO APPROACH WOMEN OF YOUR RACE!
ACTUALLY, I'M GAY.
WHAT KIND OF GAY RACIST ARE YOU?
TED RALL
CHRONICLE FEATURES

IF YOU DON'T HAVE ANYTHING NICE TO SAY, DON'T SAY ANYTHING AT ALL.
©1990 TED RALL

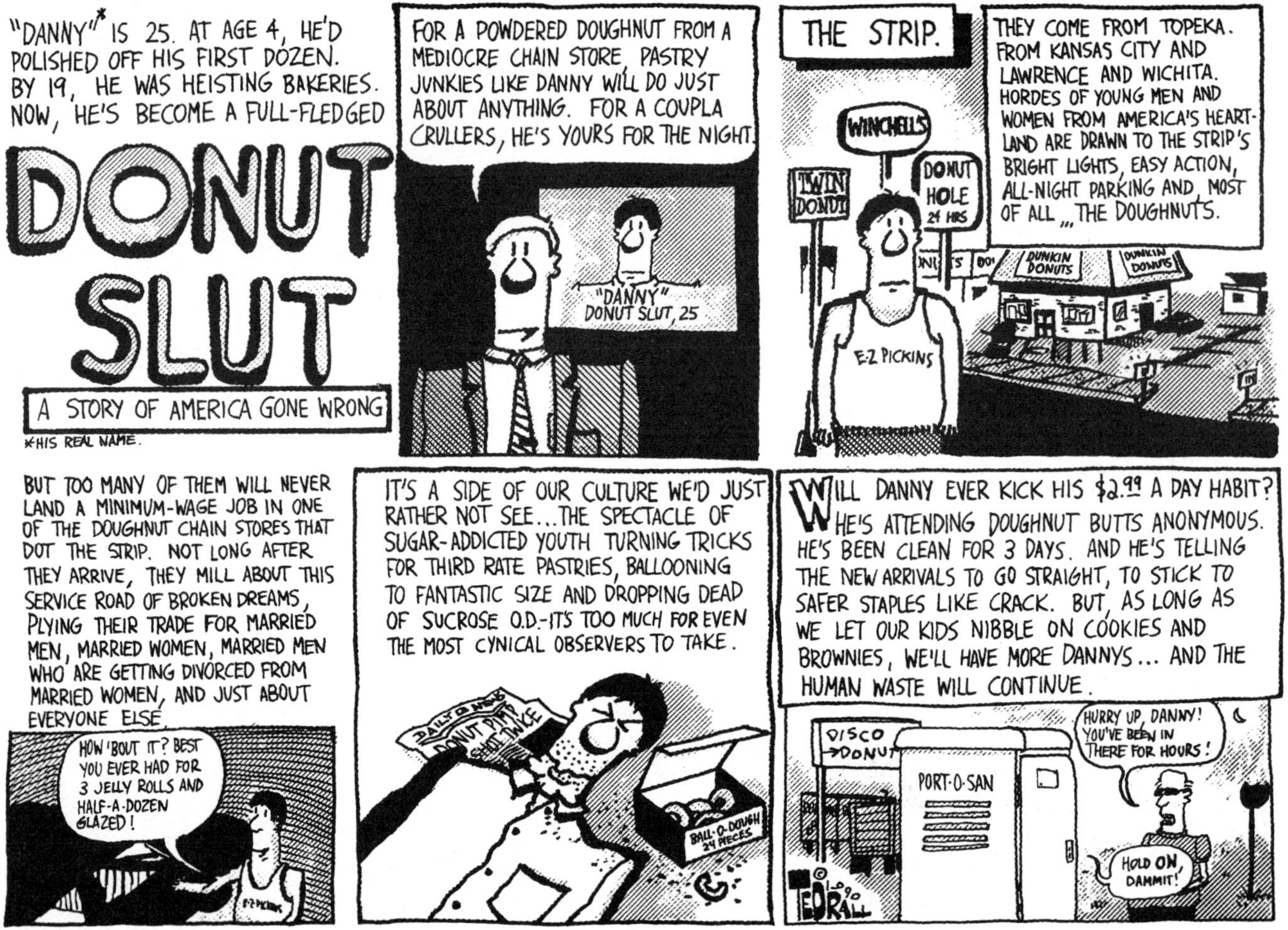
"DANNY"* IS 25. AT AGE 4, HE'D POLISHED OFF HIS FIRST DOZEN. BY 19, HE WAS HEISTING BAKERIES. NOW, HE'S BECOME A FULL-FLEDGED
DONUT SLUT
A STORY OF AMERICA GONE WRONG
*HIS REAL NAME.
FOR A POWDERED DOUGHNUT FROM A MEDIOCRE CHAIN STORE, PASTRY JUNKIES LIKE DANNY WILL DO JUST ABOUT ANYTHING. FOR A COUPLA CRULLERS, HE'S YOURS FOR THE NIGHT.
"DANNY" DONUT SLUT, 25
THE STRIP.
THEY COME FROM TOPEKA. FROM KANSAS CITY AND LAWRENCE AND WICHITA. HORDES OF YOUNG MEN AND WOMEN FROM AMERICA'S HEART-LAND ARE DRAWN TO THE STRIP'S BRIGHT LIGHTS, EASY ACTION, ALL-NIGHT PARKING AND, MOST OF ALL ... THE DOUGHNUTS.
WINCHELL'S
TWIN DONUT
DONUT HOLE 24 HRS
DUNKIN DONUTS
DUNKIN DONUTS
E-Z PICKINS
BUT TOO MANY OF THEM WILL NEVER LAND A MINIMUM-WAGE JOB IN ONE OF THE DOUGHNUT CHAIN STORES THAT DOT THE STRIP. NOT LONG AFTER THEY ARRIVE, THEY MILL ABOUT THIS SERVICE ROAD OF BROKEN DREAMS, PLYING THEIR TRADE FOR MARRIED MEN, MARRIED WOMEN, MARRIED MEN WHO ARE GETTING DIVORCED FROM MARRIED WOMEN, AND JUST ABOUT EVERYONE ELSE.
HOW 'BOUT IT? BEST YOU EVER HAD FOR 3 JELLY ROLLS AND HALF-A-DOZEN GLAZED!
IT'S A SIDE OF OUR CULTURE WE'D JUST RATHER NOT SEE... THE SPECTACLE OF SUGAR-ADDICTED YOUTH TURNING TRICKS FOR THIRD RATE PASTRIES, BALLOONING TO FANTASTIC SIZE AND DROPPING DEAD OF SUCROSE O.D.-IT'S TOO MUCH FOR EVEN THE MOST CYNICAL OBSERVERS TO TAKE.
DAILY NEWS
DONUT PIMP SHOT TWICE
BALL-O-DOUGH 24 PIECES
WILL DANNY EVER KICK HIS $2.99 A DAY HABIT? HE'S ATTENDING DOUGHNUT BUTTS ANONYMOUS. HE'S BEEN CLEAN FOR 3 DAYS. AND HE'S TELLING THE NEW ARRIVALS TO GO STRAIGHT, TO STICK TO SAFER STAPLES LIKE CRACK. BUT, AS LONG AS WE LET OUR KIDS NIBBLE ON COOKIES AND BROWNIES, WE'LL HAVE MORE DANNYS... AND THE HUMAN WASTE WILL CONTINUE.
DISCO DONUT
PORT-O-SAN
HURRY UP, DANNY! YOU'VE BEEN IN THERE FOR HOURS!
HOLD ON, DAMMIT!
© 1990 TED RALL

TODAY'S THE DAY.
WEST
THE doors
I'M DROPPING OUT OF SCHOOL AND JOINING THE PEACE CORPS.
DEAD KENNEDYS
M.D.C.
CU
I CAN'T TAKE ANOTHER DAY AT THIS DESK. I'M QUITTING! I'LL SKIP TOWN AND OPEN MY OWN BUSINESS!
I DON'T NEED THIS STRESS! I'M PICKING UP SOME BARFLY AND RUNNING OFF WITH HER TO THE MOUNTAINS!
1 BR RIV VU SWEET
1 BR RIV VU
I'M DITCHING THIS DUMP! I'LL HOTWIRE A CAR AND DRIVE UP TO CANADA; I'LL LIVE IT UP AND FISH ALL DAY!
MT. PLEASANT HOME FOR THE AGED
TODAY'S THE DAY.
©1990
TED RALL

FELICIA TURNED 20½ THE DAY SHE REALIZED SHE DIDN'T WANT TO GROW GRAPES FOR A LIVING ON THE SAME FARM WHERE HER PARENTS' MARRIAGE HAD WITHERED UNDER THE CALIFORNIA SUN.
IT WAS THAT DAY THE RECRUITER VISITED HER SCHOOL'S SENIOR JOB FAIR.
STEVE PROMISED FELICIA EVERYTHING HIS EMPLOYER, A LOS ANGELES INSURANCE CONGLOMERATE, WOULD PERMIT HIM TO PROMISE. STEVE WAS A VERY PERSUASIVE MAN. FELICIA ACCEPTED HIS CARD.
"SURE, YOU'LL WORK LONG HOURS," STEVE SAID. "BUT YOU'LL BE SALARIED. NO ONE'LL COMPLAIN IF YOU COME IN LATE. YOU'LL BE AN INDIVIDUAL—AN INDIVIDUAL EXPECTED TO SACRIFICE PERSONAL ACTIVITIES TO PERFORM HIS—OR HER—DUTIES."
FELICIA, A FORMER DORMITORY ADVISOR, HAD NO PROBLEM WITH THIS.
SERIES 1985
"YOU'LL BE PAID THE SAME AS THE SECRETARIAL POOL AND YOU'LL HAVE MANY SECRETARIAL-TYPE DUTIES," STEVE WARNED, "BUT YOU'LL HAVE MORE RESPONSIBILITY, LONGER HOURS—YOU'LL BE PART OF MANAGEMENT."
IN
OUT
MS. MORRISON
APRIL
FELICIA, MILDLY DICTATORIAL AT HEART, WANTED VERY MUCH TO BE MANAGERIAL.
WHEN FELICIA TURNED 24, STEVE SAW HER AT THE WATER COOLER AND DISCUSSED THE IMPENDING MERGER. HE ALSO TOLD HER SHE WAS GOING TO BE PROMOTED.
"OF COURSE, YOU'LL EARN THE SAME AS SECRETARIAL POOL," STEVE COMMENTED. "BUT YOU HAVE REAL MANAGERIAL POTENTIAL WITH THE NEW COMPANY. WE'LL BE NEEDING YOU HERE ON SATURDAYS—AND SUNDAYS—AND, DESPITE YOUR TITLE, CONSIDER YOURSELF MANAGEMENT."
TED RALL ©1989

George Bush's
JOY OF ECONOMICS
HI! TODAY'S RECIPE IS "ELECTION SURPRISE". THIS SPECIAL DISH COVERS UP FOUL TASTES, EMULATES FULFILLMENT... SERVES 250,000,000 PEOPLE!
©1991 TED RALL
World's Greatest Chef
FIRST, GET ABOUT $35 BILLION IN LARGE BILLS. BUNDLE AND COUNT; ADD BORED ELECTORATE & PRESS.
APPLY GENEROUS GOBS OF PATRIOTIC RHETORIC, INANE POSTURING AND HYPOCRITICAL ACCUSATIONS...
ADD ONE RUBBER STAMP CONGRESS. (IF UNAVAILABLE, COMPLIANT LAP DOG WILL SUFFICE.)
SLAUGHTER 200 YOUNG AMERICANS AND A FEW HUNDRED THOUSAND MUSLIMS FOR TASTE...
DETONATE MIXTURE USING APPROXIMATELY ONE BILLION TONS TNT.
RECIPE REQUIRES SIX WEEKS. WHEN COOLED, STIMULATE ECONOMY WITH EXTENSIVE KITCHEN CLEAN-UP.
VIOLA! "ELECTION SURPRISE" IS READY TO SERVE. FORCE FEED TO RELUCTANT GUESTS; SATISFIES 92% OF POPULATION. REPEAT FOR BETTER RESULTS.
World's Greatest Chief

THE U.S. HAS THE HIGHEST MURDER RATE OF ANY MODERN INDUSTRIALIZED NATION...
Poppy
...THE HIGHEST INFANT MORTALITY RATE...
Poppy
...THE HIGHEST ILLITERACY RATE...
Poppy
...THE HIGHEST DISCREPANCY BETWEEN RICH AND POOR..
Poppy
...AND THE 4TH HIGHEST TAXES. BUT DON'T WORRY...
Poppy
... WE'RE WORKING ON THAT LAST ONE.
NEW TAXES

I GOT PASSED OVER FOR PROMOTION.
AT LEAST YOU STILL HAVE YOUR JOB!
I GOT FIRED.
AT LEAST YOU STILL HAVE ME!
YOU'RE LEAVING ME.
AT LEAST YOU STILL HAVE YOUR HEALTH!
AT LEAST I STILL HAVE YOUR LIFE INSURANCE!
TED RALL

JUST LOAN IT.
JUST STEAL IT.
JUST STASH IT.
JUST FUNNEL IT.
JUST LAUNDER IT.
JUST SMUGGLE IT.
JUST FUDGE IT.
JUST FINANCE IT.
JUST DON'T TALK ABOUT IT.
INTERNATIONAL BANKING: IT'S NOT JUST PENCIL-PUSHING.
TED RALL ©1991

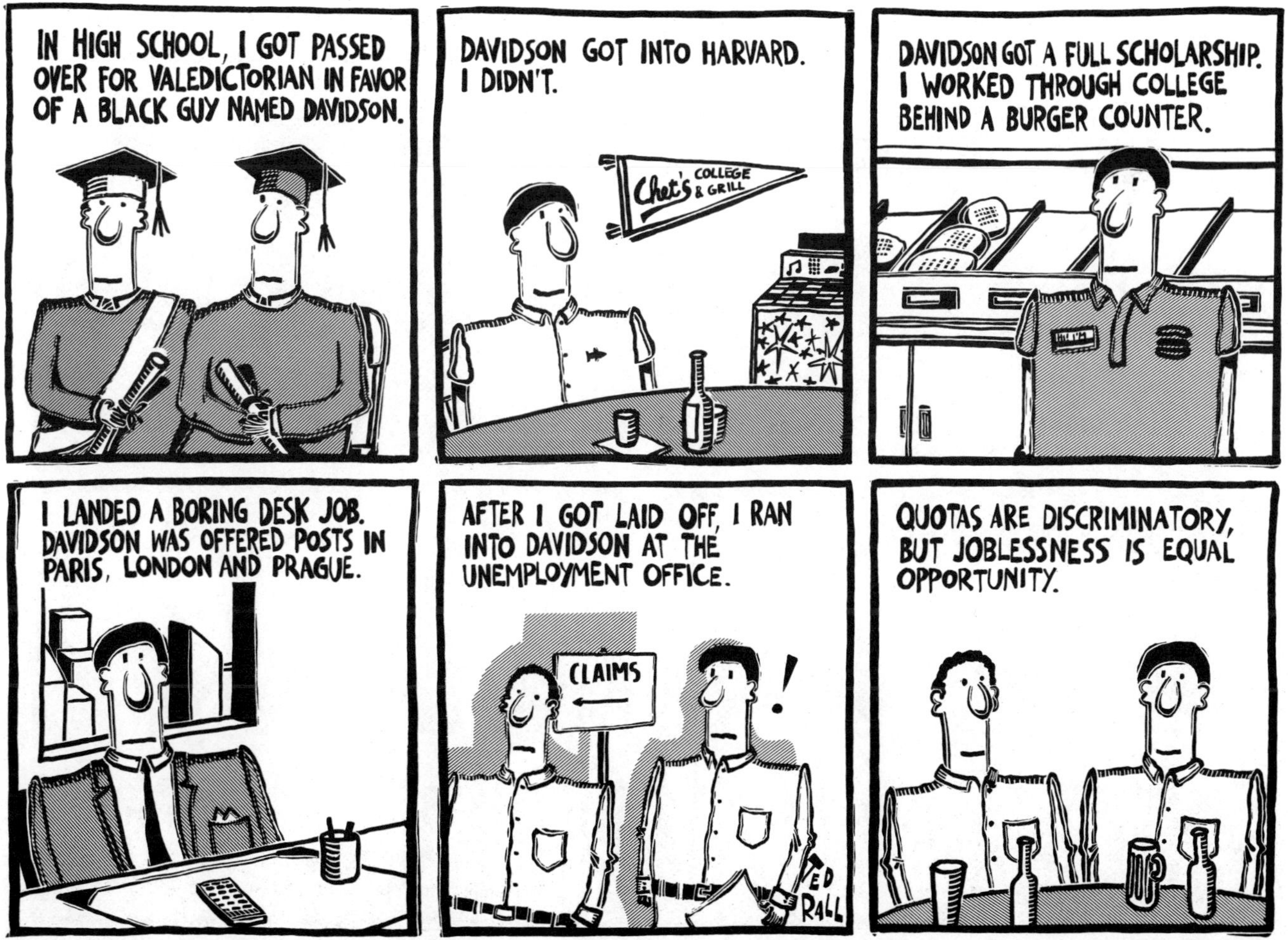
IN HIGH SCHOOL, I GOT PASSED OVER FOR VALEDICTORIAN IN FAVOR OF A BLACK GUY NAMED DAVIDSON.
DAVIDSON GOT INTO HARVARD. I DIDN'T.
Chet's COLLEGE & GRILL
DAVIDSON GOT A FULL SCHOLARSHIP. I WORKED THROUGH COLLEGE BEHIND A BURGER COUNTER.
HI, I'M
I LANDED A BORING DESK JOB. DAVIDSON WAS OFFERED POSTS IN PARIS, LONDON AND PRAGUE.
AFTER I GOT LAID OFF, I RAN INTO DAVIDSON AT THE UNEMPLOYMENT OFFICE.
CLAIMS
!
TED RALL
QUOTAS ARE DISCRIMINATORY, BUT JOBLESSNESS IS EQUAL OPPORTUNITY.

I'M GROUNDING YOU UNTIL FURTHER NOTICE. BUT, BEFORE YOU SAY ANYTHING, I WANT YOU TO TAKE A DEEP BREATH AND COUNT TO TEN.
(BREATHE) 1... 2... 3... 4... 5...
...6... 7... 8... 9... 10.
RALL ©1990
WELL?
FUCK YOU.

IT'S A GOOD THING BUSH'S TICKER IS STILL GOING... IF HE KICKS, WHO KNOWS WHAT QUAYLE WOULD DO?
IT WOULD BE SCARY...
HE MIGHT RUIN THE ECONOMY, FOR EXAMPLE... A GUY LIKE QUAYLE WOULDN'T DO A THING EVEN IF UNEMPLOYMENT AND HOMELESSNESS WERE RAMPANT!
OR HE'D GET US INTO SOME LAME WAR IN SOME COUNTRY NOBODY CAN FIND ON A MAP, OR HE'D THROW BILLIONS OF DOLLARS AT THE SAVINGS AND LOANS, OR HE'D LET EDUCATION GO TO HELL!
NOT TO MENTION APPOINTING SOME DOOFUS TO BE HIS VICE PRESIDENT!
YESSIREE, IT SURE IS COMFORTING TO KNOW THE COUNTRY'S IN GOOD HANDS!
TED RALL
© Chronicle Features, 1991

MY FATHER WAS EXEMPTED FROM PARENTHOOD BY COURT ORDER, EXCEPT FROM 1 TO 7 P.M. ON ALTERNATE SATURDAYS AND SUNDAYS.
merry
SPENCER GIFTS
SALE
MY COLLEGE PROFESSORS DIDN'T HAVE TIME TO TEACH MY CLASSES.
HI, I'M PROFESSOR McNEIL'S SUBSTITUTE'S GIRLFRIEND'S ROOMMATE, AND TODAY WE'LL BE DISCUSSING MARXISM IN A POST-INDUSTRIAL SOCIETY...
AT WORK, MY BOSS WAS SO UNOBTRUSIVE THAT NOBODY NOTICED WHEN HE DIED.
OFFICE OF THE PRESIDENT
MY LANDLORD NEVER VISITS MY BUILDING—HE DIDN'T SEE IT BEFORE HE BOUGHT IT EITHER.
6E
OF COURSE, GEORGE BUSH HAS PROVEN THAT THE COUNTRY CAN FUNCTION WITHOUT AN EXECUTIVE BRANCH.
DAILY NEWS·POST·HERALD
ECONOMY COLLAPSES
Bush: "Recovery is here!"
ABSENTEEISM—LEADERSHIP FOR THE 90s.
TED RALL

DEMOCRATIZATION FOR FUN & PROFIT
1917
1917
©1991 TED RALL

PETERS AND I HAVE BEEN ANALYZING THE PRESIDENTIAL ELECTION SYSTEM - PLEASE REFER TO YOUR REPORTS....
U.S.Corp
THE RESULTS, GENTLEMEN, ARE IN FRONT OF YOU: DISPROPORTIONATELY HIGH VOTES FOR CERTAIN STATES...
U.S.
VOTERS SO IGNORANT THEY CAN'T IDENTIFY THEIR STATE CAPITOL, AND CANDIDATES WHO AREN'T MUCH BETTER.
AVERAGE I.Q. OF PRESIDENTIAL CANDIDATES
25
0
1789
1812
1912
1944
1988
USCorp
?
BUT AFTER TOUCHING BASE WITH RESEARCH, WE'VE CONCLUDED THAT WE'RE MOVING IN THE RIGHT DIRECTION:
CHART MAINTENANCE 2%
OFFENSE 23%
DEFENSE 41%
HUMAN SERVICES 2%
MILITARY AID 15%
EDUCATION 0.4%
FARM SUBSIDIES 2%
WEAPONS MAINTENANCE 20%
UNAPPEALING CANDIDATES, AN EXCLUSIONARY TWO-PARTY SYSTEM, COMPLICATED VOTER REGISTRATION RULES, GERRYMANDERING - YES, IT'S FINALLY HAPPENED..
100%
75%
50%
25%
0
Voter Participation
1789
1812
1988
USCorp
?
WE'VE TAKEN THE PEOPLE OUT OF THE LOOP.
TED RALL

IT'S BROMIDE NIGHT AT THE
NATIONAL PLATITUDE HOTLINE
OKAY, SO YOUR HUSBAND BEATS YOU. JUST REMEMBER: WHAT GOES AROUND COMES AROUND!
I KNOW YOU EAT LITTLE KIDS..SO WHO HASN'T?
ALL RIGHT, LET'S ASSUME FOR THE SAKE OF ARGUMENT THAT YOU REALLY ARE A FAT, STUPID, CHILD-MOLESTING DOPE FIEND: YOU HAVE TO LOVE YOURSELF BEFORE YOU CAN TURN YOUR LIFE AROUND!
© Chronicle Features, 1992
TED RALL

IT ALL STARTED WITH A SIMPLE LIE TO MAKE LIFE EASIER
THEN I LIED TO COVER FOR THAT LIE
AND LIED SOME MORE TO COVER UP THOSE LIES
UNTIL I SPUN A VAST WEB OF DECEIT THAT NO ONE COULD POSSIBLY CONTROL
I'M BORN TO LEAD.
TED RALL

BEFORE I CAN PROCESS YOUR APPLICATION FOR EMPLOYMENT, I NEED TO ASK YOU IF YOU'VE EVER DONE DRUGS OR STOLEN ANYTHING.
NOPE.
DO YOU ENGAGE IN UNUSUAL SEXUAL PRACTICES? ARE YOU A HOMOSEXUAL? A CHRISTIAN? WHAT'S YOUR FAVORITE TV PROGRAM?
UH-HUH. NAH. MMM-HMMM. "SPEED RACER."
DO YOU LOVE YOUR MOTHER? DO YOU SLEEP IN THE NUDE? HAVE YOU EVER PULLED OFF THE WINGS OF A FLY? DO YOU LIKE SKIM MILK?
PARDON ME, BUT I CAN'T SEE WHAT THESE QUESTIONS HAVE TO DO WITH THE JOB FOR WHICH I'M APPLYING...
HAVE YOU EVER HAD AN UNNATURAL ATTRACTION TO HAMBURGER MEAT? WOULD YOU RATHER HAVE SEX OR DEEP-FRY?

YOU KNOW, DAN, GIRLS WOULD LIKE YOU BETTER IF YOU TOOK THEM TO NICER PLACES.
TOM'S REST
© Chronicle Features, 1991
AND THEIR PARENTS WOULD RESPECT YOU A LOT MORE IF YOU HAD A PRESTIGIOUS JOB.
NO STANDING ANYTIME
US MAIL
LOOK AT THESE GEEKY CLOTHES! OH, AND PLEASE BAG THAT HOKEY ACCENT.
YOU'VE GOT TO BUY A COOL CAR, TOO. WOMEN DON'T LIKE TO TAKE THE BUS ON A DATE.
WHY AREN'T YOU MORE ATHLETIC? GIRLS LIKE GUYS WHO ARE IN GOOD SHAPE.
ALSO, YOU SHOULD BE MORE SELF-CONFIDENT. WOMEN DON'T LIKE INSECURE MEN.
TED RALL

THIS AFTERNOON, THE REPUBLICAN NATIONAL COMMITTEE ANNOUNCED ITS INTENTION TO ACQUIRE THE DEMOCRATIC PARTY.
BUSINESS WATCH
LEE ATWATER, THE G.O.P.'S GUITAR-WIELDING, DECEASED PARTY CHAIRMAN, SAID: "THIS IS NOT A HOSTILE TAKEOVER. WE'VE BEEN WORKING TOGETHER FOR 12 YEARS ANYWAY."
BOTH PARTIES' ORGANIZATIONS WILL BE MERGED INTO THE NEW "UNIPARTY" NEXT WEEK.
WALL STREET REACTED WITH A SHRUG. ONE ANALYST QUIPPED: "OLD NEWS." THE DEMOCRATS, FOUNDED IN 1830, PASSED TITLE TO THEIR EX-RIVALS AT NO COST, NOTING THAT THEY HAD SOLD OUT YEARS BEFORE. THE NATION'S POLITICAL AFFAIRS ARE EXPECTED TO BE HANDLED WITH INCREASED EFFICIENCY AFTER THE MERGER.
WHAT ABOUT THE DEMOCRATS' ASSETS? EVERYTHING WILL BE SOLD THAT IS USELESS, INCLUDING THEIR MEMBERS. THE CONVENTIONS, HOWEVER, WILL CONTINUE. AS ONE REPUBLICAN OFFICIAL SAID, "THEY ALWAYS CHOOSE MORE INTERESTING CITIES."
TED RALL

IF YOU LIVED HERE
YOU'D BE HOME
BY NOW
© Chronicle Features, 1991
TED RALL

WAR!
12
13
I'M NOT AFRAID TO DIE.
©1991 TOM TOMORROW

SORRY, PAL... I'D LOVE TO HELP YOU OUT, BUT I JUST BLEW ALL MY CHANGE ON A CAN OF DOG FOOD FOR A STRAY. I CAN'T STAND THE SIGHT OF A HUNGRY DOG!
HOMELESS PLEASE HELP
LOOK, ENOUGH IS ENOUGH! THIS ANIMAL TESTING HAS GOT TO STOP!
HOMELESS
Phone
Phone
911
I COULDN'T BELIEVE IT! $750 IN VET'S BILLS!
HOMELESS
ARF! ARF!
TED RALL © 1990

THE DEATH OF
FRED BASSET
PUT A MOVE ON, YOU INSIPID, POORLY-DRAWN SLAB OF TRITE BANALITY!
I'm published, therefore I am.
DON'T FORGET YOUR PLACE, DOG! ANIMAL RIGHTS OR NOT, YOUR COPYRIGHTED BUTT IS MINE!
MAYBE WHAT YOU NEED IS SOME *@*@* DISCIPLINE!
OH, MY GOD! FRED, YOU'VE FINALLY FLIPPED! YOU'RE NUTS! PLEASE STOP! THIS IS A CHILDREN'S STRIP, DAMMIT!
Eat death, scum (chomp, chew, gnash, gnaw)
OH, FUDGE. I'VE KILLED HIM.
But who can tell?
TED RALL

PEACE!
ENCH FRIES 89¢
ESEBURGER $5.95 PLUS TAX
OFFOMEGADOG $1.99
SPECIAL
NOW WHAT?
©1991 TED RALL

CIVIL RIGHTS, FREEDOM RIDERS, THE FREE SPEECH MOVEMENT, THE BLACK PANTHERS, THE HIPPIES, COMMUNES, FREE LOVE, ALLAN GINSBERG, THE 1968 CHICAGO DEMOCRATIC CONVENTION, SDS, KENT STATE, FEMINISM, THE UNDERGROUND PRESS, HAIGHT-ASHBURY, THE WEATHERMEN, HO CHI MINH, MY LAI, LBJ, YIPPIES, BIRTH CONTROL PILLS, THE GENERATION GAP, NIXON,
DYLAN, THE BEATLES, THE STONES, THE DOORS, THE GRATEFUL DEAD, JEFFERSON AIRPLANE, THE SEEDS, THE KINKS, WOODSTOCK, CCR, THE YARDBIRDS, THE ANIMALS, JAMES BROWN, THE SUPREMES, THE FOUR TOPS, ARETHA FRANKLIN, THE BYRDS, THE BEACH BOYS, THE ELVIS COMEBACK TOUR, PHIL SPECTOR, THE JACKSON 5, THE VELVET UNDERGROUND, THE PRETTY THINGS,
HELL'S ANGELS, LSD, BARRY GOLDWATER, ALTAMONT, THE PRAGUE SPRING, JOAN BAEZ, BAY OF PIGS, DR. SPOCK, THE DAYS OF RAGE, WALLACE, RFK, MALCOLM X, MARTIN LUTHER KING, JR., ABBIE HOFFMAN, HASH, MAY 1968, JEAN-PAUL SARTRE, TOM WOLFE, CHE GUEVARA, CULTURAL REVOLUTION, MUHAMMED ALI, ELDRIDGE CLEAVER, CHICAGO 8,
THE NEW REALISM, THE ECONOMIC RECOVERY OF 1983-86, A NEW MORNING IN AMERICA, PULLING ONE'S SELF BY HIS/HER BOOTSTRAPS, MBA'S, MALAISE, DRAFT REGISTRATION, CONFORMITY, THE NEW CELIBACY, AIDS, THE END OF IDEALISM, BACK TO BASICS, THE CRISIS IN EDUCATION, JAMES WATT, AL HAIG, ED MEESE, GEORGE BUSH, LOOKING OUT FOR NO. 1, CONSUMERISM,
"THE WONDER YEARS," "THIRTYSOMETHING," "STAND BY ME," MINISKIRTS, FLOWERED SHIRTS, BOHEMIAN CHIC, THE BABY BOOMER MARKET, NORMAN MAILER, JIMMY BRESLIN, YUPPIES, "GUPPIES", BMW'S DAY-GLO, WARH AGAN, WILL MISM, THE NE FEIFFER, CAREERISM, THE VILLAGE VOICE, NOAM CHOMSKY, REAGAN AND OTHER 60'S NOSTALGIA
YOU KNOW WHAT YOUR GENERATION'S PROBLEM IS?
YOU'VE GOT NOTHING TO SAY.
©1991 TED RALL

SHE SPENDS HER DAYS THINKING OF WAYS TO ORDER ME AROUND
THEN SHE CRITICIZES EVERY MOVE I MAKE
AND SHE VETOES ALL MY ATTEMPTS TO HAVE FUN
WHILE DERIDING MY INABILITY TO ASSERT MYSELF.
SO WHY DON'T I LEAVE?
I CAN'T IMAGINE LIFE WITHOUT HER.
© 1990 RALL ED

I DON'T HAVE TO LIE!
I DON'T HAVE TO CHEAT!
I DON'T HAVE TO STEAL!
I DON'T HAVE TO HURT ANYONE!
I'M FREE!
I'M BORED.
© TED 1990 RALL

I'VE HEARD TOO MANY SPEECHES.
I'VE READ TOO MANY BOOKS.
I'VE SEEN TOO MANY MOVIES.
I'VE LISTENED TO TOO MUCH MUSIC.
I'VE ABSORBED SO MUCH INFORMATION THAT I CAN'T THINK.
I'VE THOUGHT SO MUCH THAT I CAN'T MOVE.
STUPIDITY ISN'T INHERITED.
IT'S LEARNED.
©1991 CHRONICLE FEATURES
TEIRALL

8-13

FIRST YOU TOLD ME TO FINISH COLLEGE, BUT YOU DIDN'T GIVE ME A DIME.
THEN YOU TOLD ME TO GET A GOOD JOB, BUT YOUR GENERATION KEPT ALL THE GOOD JOBS FOR THEMSELVES.
NOW YOU WANT ME TO GET MARRIED, DESPITE THE FACT THAT YOU AND ALL OF MY FRIENDS' PARENTS ARE DIVORCED.
WHEN ARE YOU GOING TO GROW UP?
TED RALL ©1991

HE'S SO SENSITIVE.
HE ALWAYS ASKS ME HOW I AM.
HE GOES WITH ME TO THE MUSEUM AND HIS FRIENDS GO PLAY BALL WITHOUT HIM.
HE ISN'T AFRAID TO KISS ME IN PUBLIC.
I HAVE NEVER MET A KINDER, MORE CONSIDERATE MAN IN MY LIFE.
GEEK.
©1990 TED RALL

YOUR POCKET GUIDE TO U.S. ECONOMICS

BOOM

(a.k.a. GOOD TIMES, PROSPERITY, UPSWING, HALYCON TIMES, BULL MARKET, TIME O'PLENTY)

How to identify: Only the poor suffer.

Frequency: Twice per century.

Duration: 5 to 15 years.

Causes: War; previous depression.

Advice: Grin, enjoy, be arrogant. Earn money in exploitative company while you can.

TED RALL © 1991

RECESSION

(a.k.a. SLUMP, DOWNTURN, CORRECTION, TEMPORARY ADJUSTMENT, CAUTIOUS CLIMATE, SETBACK, HARD TIMES, DECLINE, BEAR MARKET, DEFINITELY-ABSOLUTELY-POSITIVELY-NOT-A-DEPRESSION)

How to identify: The middle class suffer.

Frequency: Every 8 to 9 years.

Duration: 2 to 10 years.

Causes: Previous boom; Republicans.

Advice: Worry, agonize. Cheat on your taxes.

DEPRESSION

(a.k.a. FREEFALL, COLLAPSE, DEATH-ON-A-PLATE, THE-END-OF-THE-WORLD-AS-WE-KNOW-IT, JUST-A-RECESSION, TIME-OF-REASSESSMENT, THE SKIDS)

How to identify: The rich suffer.

Frequency: Twice per century.

Duration: 10 years.

Causes: Previous recession; Republicans with successful reelections.

Advice: Invest in alcohol, drugs and firearms. Dance.

THEY WERE THE BYPRODUCTS OF A WARTIME EXPERIMENT GONE AWRY. LITTLE DID THE WORLD KNOW WHAT HORROR WOULD BE UNLEASHED BY
C.H.I.A.
(Cutesy Humongous Invertebrate Animals)
©1990
A TALE OF LOUSY URBAN PLANNING BY TED RALL
IT STARTED INNOCENTLY ENOUGH. VENTURE CAPITALISTS, EAGER TO IMPROVE SALES OF THEIR LATEST GIMMICK, PERUSED RECENTLY DECLASSIFIED GOVERNMENT REPORTS. SOON, THEY WERE ABLE TO GO TO MARKET WITH THEIR AWESOME IMPROVEMENT ON THE FAMILIAR CUDDLY DENIZENS OF LATE-NIGHT TELEVISION:
BUY THE NEW "IMPROVED" Chia Pet! WATCH ITS FUR GROW OUT DAY AFTER DAY... JUST ADD WATER AND ENJOY! (NO PERVERTS PLEASE)
$9.95
HUNDREDS OF INNER CITY PARENTS, UNABLE TO AFFORD MORE UPSCALE LIVE PETS, COMMITTED $9.95 EACH TO GET THE ADORABLE, DEHYDRATED CHIAS FOR THEIR CHILDREN.
HERE, SWEETIE. THIS BEAUTIFUL, FAITHFUL LOW-COST COMPANION WILL PROVIDE YOU WITH HOURS OF FUN AND FRIENDSHIP WHILE YOUR MOTHER AND I WORK THE TRIPLE NIGHT SHIFT DOWN AT THE BIOLOGICAL WARFARE LAB!
SLUM SWEET
THANK YOU, FATHER. NOW I WILL GROW UP TO BE A REASONABLY WELL-ADJUSTED LOWER MIDDLE CLASS ADULT, THANKS TO THIS ENVIRONMENTALLY DUBIOUS TOY!
VIRTUALLY SAFE! NEW CHIA PET
CLASS
EVENTUALLY, OF COURSE, THE INEVITABLE HAPPENED...
MOMMY, CHIA'S BIG AND ICKY!
DON'T WORRY, HONEY THAT HORRIBLE THING WON'T BOTHER YOU ANYMORE!
FOOOSH!
THE FORMER CHIA CHUMS FOUND THEMSELVES DEEP IN THE BOWELS OF THE ANCIENT CITY SEWER SYSTEM, WHERE PEELED LEAD LINING FROM OLD PIPES, YEARS OF TOXIC WASTE DUMPING AND AN ENDLESS SUPPLY OF WATER CONSPIRED TO TRANSMOGRIFY THEM INTO SOMETHING VERY DIFFERENT...
SAY, ARTIE, AIN'T THE "D" TRAIN SUPPOSED TO COME IN ANOTHER 45 MINUTES? ARTIE?.. ARTIE?
URP
MTA
THE ENORMOUS C.H.I.A.S PROWL THE NETWORK OF SEWER LINES AND SUBWAY TUNNELS BENEATH THE CITY, BALLOONING TO FANTASTIC PROPORTIONS, FRENZIED IN THEIR CONSTANT SEARCH FOR THEIR ONLY ACCEPTABLE SOURCE OF NOURISHMENT–
–HUMAN FLESH COATED BY A THIN LAYER OF POLYESTER.
TY POLI E
...THANKFULLY, ALL THE VICTIMS HAVE BEEN SUBURBANITES.
YES–BUT FOR HOW LONG? FOR HOW LONG?
MAYOR
COUNCILMAN
LA FIN?

WHEN CIVILITY GOES TOO FAR

BY TED RALL

SENIOR CITIZENS ARE ONLY 13% OF THE POPULATION AND RECEIVE 29% OF FEDERAL SPENDING. BUT AMERICANS UNDER AGE 18 GET ONLY 7% EVEN THOUGH THERE ARE OVER TWICE AS MANY OF THEM.
THANKS TO RUTHLESS LOBBYING, OLDER AMERICANS GOT THE G.I. BILL, LOW-INTEREST MORTGAGES, SOCIAL SECURITY AND MEDICARE. NOW THAT THEY GOT THEIRS, THEY DON'T WANT TO PAY A DIME FOR PUBLIC WORKS OR EDUCATION!
WHY DO YOU OLD PEOPLE DO IT? WHY DO YOU PURPOSEFULLY SCREW OVER THE YOUNG JUST TO GET A FEW EXTRA BUCKS?
EATING YOU ISN'T LEGAL.
TED RALL ©1991 CHRONICLE FEATURES

LAST QUARTER, OUR FIRM RECORDED ITS BIGGEST PROFITS EVER! 'COURSE, EVERYONE WANTS TO KNOW HOW I DID IT...
TRUTH IS, IT WAS EASY! I LAID OFF 15,000 EMPLOYEES, FORCED 2,000 TO TAKE AN EARLY RETIREMENT AND CUT THE SALARIES OF THOSE WHO STAYED. PROFITS SOARED! STOCK PRICES WENT UP 35%—NOT BAD FOR A RECESSION, HUH?
IN THE LONG RUN, OF COURSE, ALL THOSE LAYOFFS AND LOW SALARIES TAKE THEIR TOLL, BECAUSE NOBODY'LL BE ABLE TO BUY OUR PRODUCTS! BUT BY THEN, I'LL BE GONE, SO WHO CARES, RIGHT? NONETHELESS, SOMETIMES IT IS HARD TO LIVE WITH...
THE GUILT?
NO, THE MONEY! I JUST GAVE MYSELF ANOTHER BIG RAISE, BUT WHO CAN INVEST IN THIS ECONOMY?
TED RALL © 1991

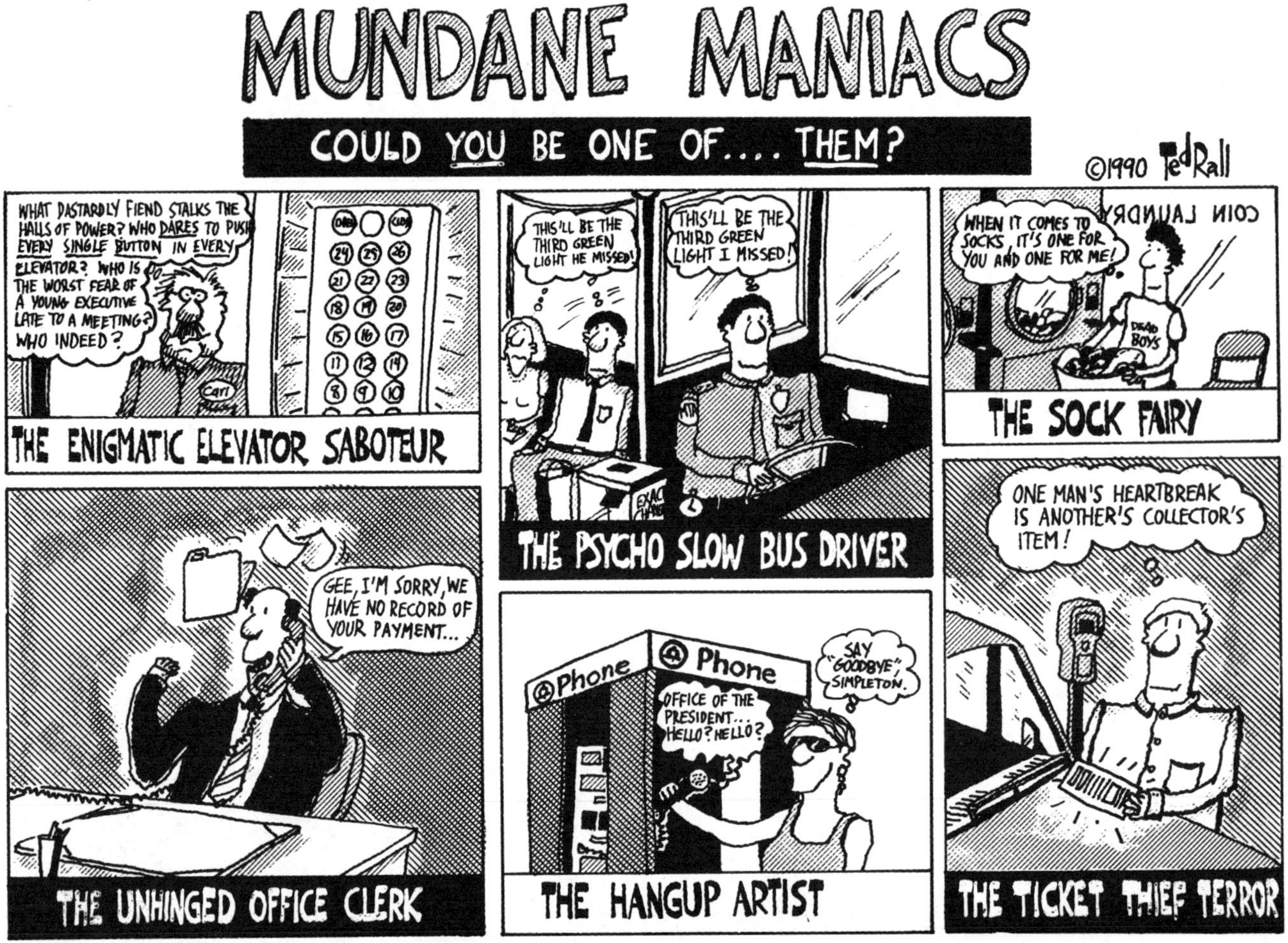
MUNDANE MANIACS
COULD YOU BE ONE OF.... THEM?
©1990 Ted Rall
WHAT DASTARDLY FIEND STALKS THE HALLS OF POWER? WHO DARES TO PUSH EVERY SINGLE BUTTON IN EVERY ELEVATOR? WHO IS THE WORST FEAR OF A YOUNG EXECUTIVE LATE TO A MEETING? WHO INDEED?
THE ENIGMATIC ELEVATOR SABOTEUR
THIS'LL BE THE THIRD GREEN LIGHT HE MISSED!
THIS'LL BE THE THIRD GREEN LIGHT I MISSED!
THE PSYCHO SLOW BUS DRIVER
WHEN IT COMES TO SOCKS, IT'S ONE FOR YOU AND ONE FOR ME!
DEAD BOYS
THE SOCK FAIRY
GEE, I'M SORRY, WE HAVE NO RECORD OF YOUR PAYMENT...
THE UNHINGED OFFICE CLERK
Phone
Phone
OFFICE OF THE PRESIDENT... HELLO? HELLO?
SAY "GOODBYE," SIMPLETON.
THE HANGUP ARTIST
ONE MAN'S HEARTBREAK IS ANOTHER'S COLLECTOR'S ITEM!
THE TICKET THIEF TERROR

SHE HAS NO INTEREST IN ME WHATSOEVER.
WAIT– SHE'S LOOKING AT ME!
SHE LIKES ME!
SHE... LOVES ME...
WE'LL BE TOGETHER FOREVER!
POSSESSIVE BITCH.
TED RALL © 1990

Unemployed Engineers:

WHY TAKE ANOTHER BORING JOB?

when you can train to become a

PROFESSIONAL TERROR CONSULTANT

You already know our organization. You know we get results. No matter what. But maybe you never stopped to think about exactly what goes into our work. Planning. Determination. Vision. Knowledge. Familiarity. Familiarity with plastiques. With remote-control and time-activated detonating devices. And a whole potpourri of explosives.

That's why we need people like you. If you haven't quite found the engineering job you've been looking for at a mainstream firm, perhaps you should consider us. We're looking for college-educated malcontents to staff our R&D and Planning Analysis departments, located throughout the world. If you're fascinated by thoughts of charred buildings, scattered wreckage and dismembered bodies, drop us a line.

• GOOD SALARY

• GREAT BENEFITS

ACME — Allied Conservatives Moderates And Extremists

TERROR CONSULTING INC.

Serving the business, political and goverment community since 1945

Beirut Munich Belfast Pretoria London New York Athens

"WHERE TODAY'S ENGINEERS ARE TOMORROW'S FUTURE"

TEDRALL ©1989

MY FRESHMAN YEAR IN '81, I LIKED TO LEAVE CAMPUS OFTEN.
116
116
116
NEW YORK
HEADLESS IN TOPLESS
I'D SPEND ALL DAY IN USED BOOK AND RECORD STORES, CHEAP DINERS, PUNK CLOTHING SHOPS AND FLEA MARKETS.
RAMONES
PHLEGM GLOBBERS
LIVE
THEN I'D HANG OUT ALL NIGHT AT SOME NEW WAVE NIGHTCLUB, HIT A DINER FOR BREAKFAST AND DROP INTO THE SUBWAY HOME.
UN. JULY 20TH
AT
EACON THEA
IN 1982, THOUGH, GENTRIFICATION CHANGED EVERYTHING. RENTS TRIPLED, THE STORES CLOSED, THE CLUBS WENT DISCO AND I BOUGHT A TELEVISION SET.
Sal's PIZZA
BODEGA
COMING SOON Café Societé's Low-Cal Sushi Emporium "BY APPOINTMENT ONLY"
NOW THAT I MAKE MORE THAN ENOUGH TO DO ANYTHING I WANT, THERE'S NOTHING LEFT TO DO.
TED RALL ©1989
LIVING IN NEW YORK'S LIKE A GREAT PARTY THAT'S OVER BY THE TIME YOU ARRIVE.
96

DAN BLOWS HIS INTERVIEW.

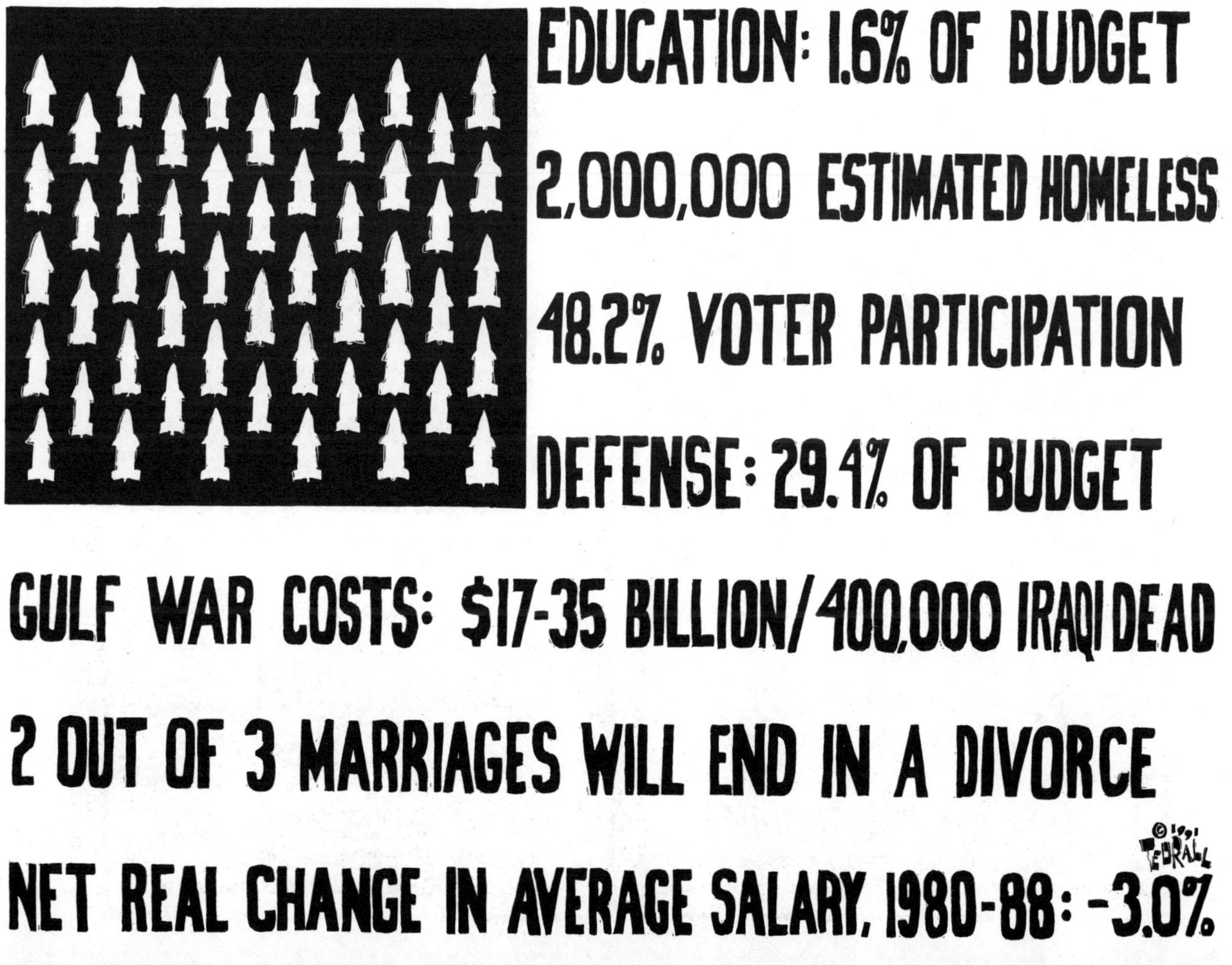
EDUCATION: 1.6% OF BUDGET
2,000,000 ESTIMATED HOMELESS
48.2% VOTER PARTICIPATION
DEFENSE: 29.4% OF BUDGET
GULF WAR COSTS: $17-35 BILLION/400,000 IRAQI DEAD
2 OUT OF 3 MARRIAGES WILL END IN A DIVORCE
NET REAL CHANGE IN AVERAGE SALARY, 1980-88: -3.0%
© 1991 TED RALL

YOUR GUIDE TO INADEQUACY
DRIVING EXAMINATIO
(1) If your car should stall on the tracks and a train is comin should you:
(a) scream
(b) scream loudly
(c) wince
(d) wince loudly
CRAPPY CAR?
CONSIDER SLITTING YOUR WRISTS!
TEDRALL ©1991
I'M 100% BEHIND THE PRESIDENT!
STUPID SPOUSE?
HOW ABOUT JUMPING IN FRONT OF A TRAIN?
DINGY, CRAMPED APARTMENT?
COMMIT A CRIME AND GET A BIGGER SPACE!
Chet's MICROWAVE
OUTDATED HOME APPLIANCES?
VOLUNTEER FOR DANGEROUS MEDICAL EXPERIMENTS TODAY!

I LOVE YOU.
GREAT!
HOW SHALL WE CONSUMMATE OUR RELATIONSHIP? THE PILL? DIAPHRAGM? I.U.D., PERHAPS?
OR HOW ABOUT THE SPONGE? CONTRACEPTIVE JELLY? I COULD ALWAYS INJECT SOME NORPLANT IN MY ARM... JUST AS LONG AS WE AVOID EACH OTHER'S DISEASES, PARASITES AND REPRODUCTIVE CELLS, WE'LL HAVE A GREAT FUTURE TOGETHER!
SEX IS SAFE, BUT LUST IS DEAD.
ISN'T MATURITY GREAT?
TED RALL

CUSTOMS →
BAGGAGE →
WELCOME TO
McUSA
18 MILLION UNEMPLOYED
45 MILLION UNDEREMPLOYED
19
TEDRALL

I CAN'T BELIEVE HOW SELFISH YOU ARE!
BABY
JUST THINK ABOUT ALL THE POLLUTION YOUR CHILD WILL PRODUCE! THINK OF THE BURDEN ON OUR RESOURCES!
BABY
IT'S PEOPLE LIKE YOU WHO ARE RUINING OUR WHOLE PLANET FOR A FEW MINUTES OF IRRESPONSIBLE PLEASURE!
BABY
WHAT ARE YOU DOING ABOUT OVERPOPULATION?
I ANNOY WOMEN SO THAT THEY'LL AVOID ME.
BABY
TED RALL
©1991 CHRONICLE FEATURES

THE SEARCH FOR WHITE IDENTITY
I TRIED TO SUPPRESS MY WHITENESS FOR YEARS... NOW I KNOW IT'S COOL TO BE COLORLESS!
THE WORLD HAS A LOT TO LEARN FROM THE FILMS OF MICHAEL J. FOX!
I, FOR ONE, AM TIRED OF LIVE BLACK WOMEN! LET'S HEAR FROM MORE DEAD WHITE GUYS IN OUR SCHOOLS!
LET'S FACE IT... WE'RE BORN TO OPPRESS!
© Chronicle Features, 1991
TEDRALL

THE WALL STREET JOURNAL
ECONOMIC RECOVERY
HIGHER UNEMPLOYMENT
TED RALL
IF I DON'T WIN THE LOTTERY, I'M GOING TO KILL MYSELF.

SOVIET JOB RETRAINING
BLUE-COLLAR VERSION
1
2
3
4
TED RALL
© Chronicle Features, 1991

HOW AFFIRMATIVE ACTION REALLY WORKS

IT'S ANOTHER THRILLING INSTALLMENT OF THE
POSTMOD SQUAD
"PURVEYORS OF JUSTICE"
WE'D BEEN LOOKING FOR THIS SCUM-BAG FOR WEEKS. FINALLY, WE GOT A LUCKY BREAK...
GREAT NEWS, CHIEF! THE SUPREME COURT JUST RULED THAT WE CAN SEARCH HOUSES WITHOUT A WARRANT IF THEIR LAWNS AREN'T PROPERLY MAINTAINED!
ALL RIGHT! WE'RE IN!
WE BROKE DOWN THE DOOR. IT WASN'T THE RIGHT GUY, BUT IT WAS THE LAST WEEK OF THE MONTH, SO WE BEAT HIM UP, IMPOUNDED HIS CAR, ROBBED HIM, ARRANGED TO HAVE HIM EVICTED AND PLANTED THE EVIDENCE WE NEEDED.
DON'T PLAY INNOCENT WITH ME, DIRTBAG! WE FOUND THAT BOOTLEG COPY OF "PRETTY WOMAN" IN THE VCR!
POLICE
HE CLAIMED INNOCENCE, BUT WE PAID OFF THE JURORS AND NABBED THE CONVICTION!
... AND SO, FOR ONE COUNT OF VIOLATION OF FEDERAL COPYRIGHT LAW, THIS COURT SENTENCES YOU TO NOT LESS THAN TWENTY YEARS IN PRISON, SO THAT AMERICA MAY BE FREE OF THE MENACE YOUR KIND REPRESENTS!
LIQUORS
STATE STORE
THE SENTENCE WAS SUSPENDED DUE TO PRISON OVERCROWDING, SO THE STATE FOUND HIM A JOB AND PAID HIM OFF QUIETLY WHEN HIS POSITION WAS CUT...
A FEW YEARS LATER, WE HEARD OUR FAVORITE EX-CON HAD MURDERED HIS EX-BOSS AND HIS EX-WIFE IN A CRACK-INDUCED FRENZY. DUE TO PRISON OVERCROWDING, HE WAS ALLOWED TO GO FREE. ONCE AGAIN, JUSTICE HAD BEEN SERVED.
NOW IF WE COULD GET THE SUPREME COURT TO RULE THAT WE CAN KILL ALL SUSPECTS...
IT'LL COME... IT'LL COME.
TED RALL
THE END

BIZARRE CONSPIRACY THEORISTS
OUR COUNTRY IS RUN BY A GROUP OF DECENT, HONEST WELL-MEANING MEN WHO TOIL CEASELESSLY TO IMPROVE OUR QUALITY OF LIFE. SURE THEY'RE UNDERPAID, BUT THEY ARE THE UNSUNG HEROES OF OUR TIME!
WE ARE SO LUCKY TO LIVE UNDER A SYSTEM THAT REWARDS ITS BRIGHTEST, MOST DECENT CITIZENS! OBVIOUSLY THOSE WHO DISAGREE WITH THE PRESIDENT ARE BITTER, LAZY, DEVIL WORSHIPERS.
©1991 CHRONICLE FEATURES
TED RALL

CONGRATULATIONS! YOU'RE QUALIFIED TO RECEIVE FINANCIAL AID!
A-C
SINCE GRANTS HAVE BEEN ELIMINATED, PLEASE COMPLETE THESE HIGH-INTEREST LOAN APPLICATIONS. IF YOU FAIL THE CREDIT CHECK, YOU'LL NEED A WEALTHY PARENT TO CO-SIGN.
I hereby agree to anything & everything
X
YOU'LL ALSO BE ELIGIBLE FOR A MINIMUM WAGE "WORK STUDY" JOB, EITHER IN THE LIBRARY SHELVING BOOKS OR IN THE CAFETERIA WASHING DISHES.
IF YOU MANAGE TO MAKE ANY MONEY DURING THE SUMMER, YOU'LL GIVE IT ALL TO US IN THE FALL SO WE CAN INVEST IN REAL ESTATE.
$
$
OF COURSE, YOUR TUITION, FEES AND COSTS WILL FAR EXCEED THE TOTAL OF YOUR FINANCIAL AID, SO WE'LL RECOMMEND SUPPLEMENTARY WORK—LIKE TUTORING—DURING TIME YOU'D OTHERWISE BE WASTING STUDYING!
ALTERNATIVE JOBS:
• CRACK DEALING
• FAST FOODOLOGY
• THEFT
• ARMED ROBBERY
WHO SAYS COLLEGE DOESN'T PREPARE YOU FOR THE REAL WORLD?
A-C
1990 JOE RALL

THEORIES FOR OUR TIMES
EVER NOTICE HOW THE DISCOVERY OF COFFEE PRECEEDED THE RENAISSANCE?
IF HUEY LEWIS REALLY ROCKED OUT, HE COULD BE REALLY GREAT!
I THINK PRESIDENT BUSH IS LIP-SYNCHED BY JACK NICHOLSON.
THE GOVERNMENT IS CUTTING BACK ON EDUCATION SO THAT AMERICANS LIKE US REMAIN UNBELIEVABLY STUPID. ALSO, ELVIS IS DEAD.
©1991 TED RALL

THE COMMON EARTHWORM.
MIRACLE OF PRIMITIVE LIFE, THE EARTHWORM EATS ITS WAY THROUGH THE SOIL AND DIRT. ITS WASTE OF DIGESTED DIRT PROVIDES VITAL NUTRIENTS. ITS DUAL GENDER PERMITS ANY TWO TO REPRODUCE IN A RITUAL UNCHANGED AFTER MILLIONS OF YEARS.
IF IT BECOMES THE VICTIM OF AN ACCIDENT AND IS CHOPPED IN TWO PIECES, THE WORM'S SIMPLE ANATOMY ALLOWS IT TO BECOME TWO SEPARATE, LIVING BEINGS.
...SO IF WE COULD DO THE SAME THING WITH DEMOCRATS, WE'D HAVE A SURE BET FOR THE WHITE HOUSE IN 1992!
DEMOCRATIC NATIONAL COMMITTEE
TED RALL

I'M NOT LEARNING ANYTHING IN SCHOOL.
SCHOOL'S NOT ABOUT LEARNING! IT'S ABOUT MONEY! JUST GET GOOD GRADES!
LYNYRD SKYNYARD
1991
YOU GET GOOD GRADES TO PROVE YOU CAN OBEY. YOU STAY OUT OF TROUBLE TO PROVE YOU CAN BE TAMED. SCHOOL TRAINS YOU FOR A LIFETIME OF CONFORMITY AND DOCILITY.
ONCE EVERY SPARK OF YOUR ORIGINALITY HAS BEEN EXTINGUISHED, YOU CAN SELL YOURSELF TO A LARGE CORPORATION WHICH WILL PAY YOU ENOUGH MONEY TO LEAD A RELATIVELY COMFORTABLE MIDDLE-CLASS EXISTENCE!
BUT NO ONE CAN FIND A JOB.
LIFE'S NOT ABOUT MONEY! IT'S ABOUT LEARNING! JUST STAY IN SCHOOL FOREVER!
THE ROLLING STONES
TED RALL

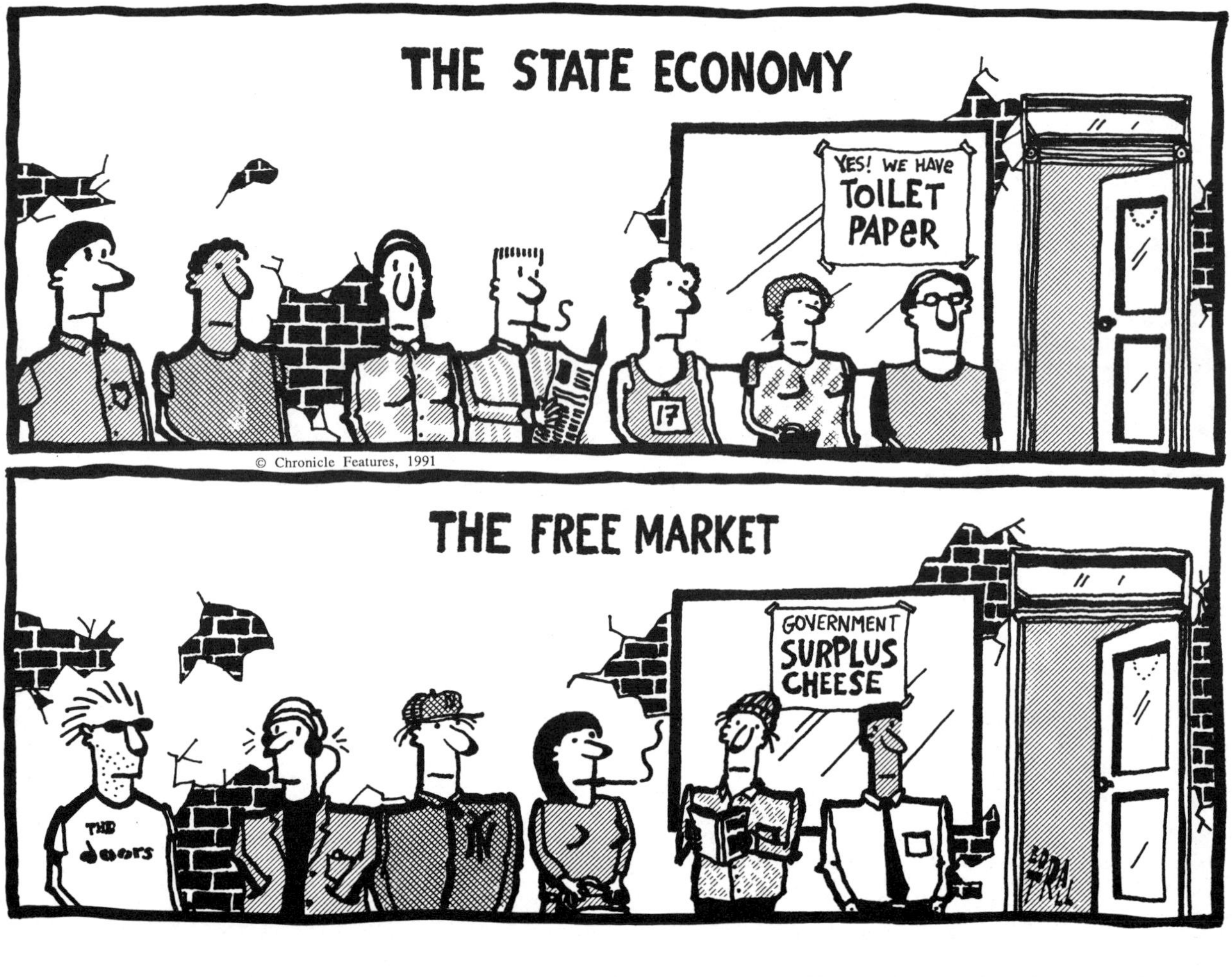
THE STATE ECONOMY
YES! WE HAVE TOILET PAPER
17
THE FREE MARKET
GOVERNMENT SURPLUS CHEESE

LIFE IS A SERIES OF PREPARATIONS...
... 12 YEARS OF BORING, REPETITIVE SCHOOLING TO PREPARE FOR 4 YEARS OF BORING, REPETITIVE COLLEGE TO PREPARE FOR ENDLESSLY BORING, REPETITIVE GRADUATE SCHOOL...
... TO PREPARE FOR A FEW MORE YEARS OF A BORING, REPETITIVE INTERNSHIP OR PERHAPS A BORING, REPETITIVE STINT AS A VOLUNTEER ...
... TO PREPARE FOR 38 YEARS OF UNEMPLOYMENT.

NEW WORLD OPTIMISM
by TED RALL © 1991
I SPEND MORE TIME WITH MY FAMILY AND FRIENDS SINCE I LOST MY JOB!
MY SON'S DEATH IN IRAQ HAS BEEN A REAL WINDFALL... CAN'T BEAT THAT LIFE INSURANCE!
NO MORE CONFLICTS BETWEEN MY CAREER AND MY PERSONAL LIFE... NOW I CAN'T AFFORD EITHER ONE!
IF I HAD MONEY, I COULD SCORE A GREAT HOUSE IN THIS DEPRESSED MARKET!
UNEMPLOYMENT BENEFITS

HAVE YOU EVER TRIED TO MAKE A LIST OF ALL THE REASONS TO GO ON LIVING...
MEN
...AND HAD NOTHING COME TO MIND?
This is art.
NEVER.
©1990 TED RALL

IT'S ABOUT TIME THAT THE WORLD RECOGNIZE THAT WE MEAN WELL!
GERMANS AND AUSTRIANS WANT ONLY PEACE!
GERMANY
AUSTRIA
WE AREN'T TRYING TO TAKE OVER EUROPE. WE'RE ACCEPTING OUR ROLES AS LEADERS.
OUR DARK PAST IS OVER! WE'RE NO LONGER NAZIS, YOU KNOW.
HEE, HEE, HEE.
GROSSE
DEUTSCHLAND

FRIENdShiP for ACCOUNTants
WILL YOU DO ME A FAVOR?
ALTHOUGH YOU DID ME SEVERAL FAVORS IN THE PAST, THEY'VE DEPRECIATED DOWN TO NOTHING. I CAN, HOWEVER, ADVANCE YOU A SMALL MINI-FAVOR ON CREDIT AT PRIME + 2% ON THE CONDITION THAT YOU RECIPROCATE WITHIN A YEAR.
© Chronicle Features, 1992
TED RALL

I'M SORRY, GENTLEMEN, BUT WE SHOW NO RECORD OF YOUR RESERVATIONS.
Le Poison Vert
OH, WOW...
ARE YOU SURE?
QUITE SURE, SIR.
I'M BEGINNING TO UNDERSTAND THE DREADFUL AGONY OF NOT KNOWING WHERE YOUR NEXT MEAL IS COMING FROM.
NO DOUBT. WANNA GO FOR SUSHI INSTEAD?
TELNAES
© Chronicle Features, 1992

CF 012092-C

SIX MONTHS AGO, THE UNITED STATES DROPPED TENS OF THOUSANDS OF BOMBS ON IRAQ, THEN INVADED AND SHOT THE REMAINING SOLDIERS AS THEY FLED. PRESIDENT BUSH DECLARED VICTORY.
NEWS
NOW THE REAL PROBLEMS BEGIN. SADDAM HUSSEIN'S STILL IN POWER; BOTH KUWAIT AND IRAQ ARE IN RUINS. WHAT IRONY!
TED RALL
TEN YEARS AGO, REAGAN DEREGULATED BANKING, REAL ESTATE AND THE AIRLINES. AS STOCKS ZOOMED UP IN VALUE, ECONOMISTS CALLED THE '80s THE LONGEST PERIOD OF SUSTAINED GROWTH IN U.S. HISTORY!
NEWS
WHO COULD HAVE GUESSED THAT TODAY, THOSE SAME POLICIES ARE BLAMED FOR RUINING THE ECONOMY? NOT US, THAT'S FOR SURE!
HALF A CENTURY AGO, MIDDLE-CLASS AMERICANS BEGAN A MASS MIGRATION TO THE SUBURBS. THEIR QUEST FOR INEXPENSIVE, SAFE HOUSING WAS SEEN AS THE ULTIMATE REALIZATION OF THE AMERICAN DREAM.
NEWS
LITTLE COULD THEY HAVE KNOWN THEY'D HAVE TO PAY HIGHER TAXES TO POLICE THE CITIES THEY'D ABANDONED OR THAT THEIR KIDS WOULD GROW UP SO BORED THEY WOULD BECOME SUICIDAL DRUGGIES! WHAT A SURPRISE!
ALMOST SEVENTY YEARS AGO, VLADIMIR ZWORYKIN INVENTED THE ICONOSCOPE, THE PREDECESSOR TO THE MODERN TELEVISION. SINCE THEN, BROADCASTERS HAVE INSIPIDLY INSISTED ON READING THE NEWS WITHOUT VENTURING ANY INSIGHTS WHATSOEVER. THAT WAY, EVERYTHING THEY SAY SEEMS SURPRISING, EVEN THOUGH IT'S ALL PREDICTABLE!
NEWS
AMAZINGLY, PEOPLE STILL PREFER TO GET THEIR NEWS FROM TV THAN FROM NEWSPAPERS! SURPRISING, TO SAY THE LEAST!

12 REASONS TO KILL YOUR PARENTS
1 IT'D BE EASY.
SIMPLY CONCENTRATE ON ONE GRUDGE AGAINST EACH PARENT; AIM CAREFULLY AND SQUEEZE TRIGGER.
2 YOU'D GET AWAY WITH IT.
3505
WITH ALL THE REAL CRIME GOING ON, THE POLICE WOULDN'T HAVE TIME TO BOTHER WITH PATRICIDE AND/OR MATRICIDE.
3 YOU WOULDN'T BE PUNISHED.
IF YOU WERE STUPID ENOUGH TO GET CAUGHT, YOU COULD GET A DECENT LAWYER TO CLAIM TEMPORARY INSANITY.
4 YOU WOULDN'T MISS THEM.
YOU HAVEN'T LOVED THEM IN YEARS; YOU ONLY SEE THEM TO FEED YOUR PRIMORDIAL GUILT OR TO GET IDEAS FOR A NEW BOOK.
5 YOUR FINANCIAL TROUBLES WOULD BE OVER.
SUBURBAN HOME FOR SALE
IMAGINE THE WINDFALL: LIFE INSURANCE, HOME, CAR, FURNITURE, JEWELRY, CASH, STOCKS, BONDS... ALL YOURS!
6 NO MORE ANNOYING LONG PHONE CALLS.
Z
REMEMBER ALL THOSE SUNDAY NIGHTS WASTED LISTENING TO YOUR PARENTS DRONE ON AND ON AND ON? NO MORE!
7 NO MORE WEEKENDS IN THE SUBURBS.
YOUR QUALITY OF LIFE WOULD IMPROVE EVERY WEEKEND THAT YOU SPEND AWAY FROM BORING PEOPLE AND PLACES—LIKE HOME!
8 IT WOULD BE GOOD FOR YOUR SANITY.
NO MORE PARENT-INDUCED STRESS SEXUAL DYSFUNCTIONS OR FINANCIAL MANIPULATION... IT'S 6 BULLETS TO A BETTER LIFE!
9 IT WOULD BE GOOD FOR THE ENVIRONMENT.
KNOCKING OFF MOM AND DAD WOULD SAVE OXYGEN, LANDFILL SPACE, FOOD SUPPLIES AND NATURAL RESOURCES... WHILE PROVIDING MUCH-NEEDED MULCH!
10 IT WOULD HELP THE ECONOMY.
THE WALL STREET JOURNAL
DOW HITS 6,000: UNEMPLOYMENT PLUNGES TO 0.1%.
IF EVERYONE MURDERED THE OLD FARTS, IT WOULD SAVE THE SOCIAL SECURITY SYSTEM, REDUCE UNEMPLOYMENT, INCREASE AVERAGE INCOME AND THE COUNTRY WOULD SHIFT TO THE LEFT!
11 WHY THE HELL NOT?
I DUNNO.
IT'S HARD TO ARGUE – THE "MORAL" PROHIBITION AGAINST KILLING YOUR FOLKS IS AN INVENTION OF – YOU GUESSED IT – OLD PEOPLE!
12 YOU COULD FINALLY AFFORD TO HAVE KIDS.
© 1991 TED RALL
WITH ALL THAT EXTRA CASH, YOU COULD FINALLY HAVE KIDS! (CAUTION: DO NOT SHOW THEM THIS CARTOON!!)

I REFUSE TO SELL OUT.
I'D RATHER BE POOR MY ENTIRE LIFE THAN DO SOMETHING I DON'T BELIEVE IN.
THE DAY I FOREGO MY ETHICS IS THE DAY I DIE.
THERE ISN'T ENOUGH MONEY IN THE WHOLE WORLD TO GET ME TO COMPROMISE MYSELF.
SIGN HERE, PLEASE.
OK.
FAME! FORTUNE! $$$
I REFUSE TO SELL OUT COMPLETELY.
©1991 TED RALL